THE ULTIMATE GUIDE TO MAKE YOUR SALARY LAST BEYOND 15TH.

SIMPLE STRATEGIES FOR BUDGETING, MANAGING, AND SAVING THE MAXIMUM FROM YOUR SALARY

PRATIK SONAR

Clever Fox®
PUBLISHING
Chennai • Bangalore

CLEVER FOX PUBLISHING
Chennai, India

Published by CLEVER FOX PUBLISHING 2025

ISBN: 978-93-6707-633-0

I would like to thank my wife, mother, father, sister and my son for encouraging me through all the thick and thin to write this book.

To all the men and women who rise each day, face every challenge, and bear every burden with quiet strength—only to provide for their families, no matter the odds.

This book is a salute to your resilience, your sacrifices, and your unwavering love.

CONTENTS

PROLOGUE

Money is a funny character. It arrives dressed like a king, with trumpets and fanfare, usually on the first of the month. The moment your bank sends that little notification—"₹50,000 credited"—you feel like the hero of your own story. Suddenly, every café seems affordable, every wishlist item feels within reach, and the month ahead looks like a smooth drive on a wide highway. For a few hours, sometimes even a few days, life feels comfortable. Then slowly, stealthily, the money sneaks away. One impulse order here, one forgotten subscription there, a sudden party, a friend's birthday, a cab ride you justified because it was raining—and by the time the calendar flips to the twentieth, you're scratching your head, wondering where it all went.

It's the universal mystery of the disappearing salary. Ask around. The intern fresh out of college feels it. The mid-career professional with a six-figure income feels it. Even the so-called "well-settled" family feels it. The number in your account may change, but the story doesn't. Money, when left without a plan, is like sand in your hands—the tighter you grip, the faster it slips away. We joke about it all the time. Memes about being broke by the fifteenth. The collective sigh of colleagues who know that the first week of the month is "treat week" and the last week is "who's bringing tiffin?" week. But beneath the jokes lies a very real stress. Financial stress. The kind that gnaws at the back of your mind, even when you're laughing at a movie or enjoying dinner with friends. The kind that makes you open your banking app three times a day, as if the balance will magically increase if you just look at it often enough.

Here's the truth: managing money is harder than earning it. Schools don't teach it. Offices don't discuss it. Families often avoid it. And so, we stumble into adulthood thinking that income alone will solve our problems. We chase increments, we change jobs, we hunt side hustles—all in the belief that "more money" will equal "less worry." But reality is less flattering. If you don't know how to handle ₹30,000, you won't magically handle ₹80,000. In fact, you might just upgrade your problems. Bigger salary, bigger lifestyle, bigger chaos. This book was born out of that chaos. But instead of treating money like a monster to be tamed, it treats it like a partner to be understood. Not with lectures. Not with guilt trips. Not with spreadsheets that make you feel like you need an MBA just to survive. No, this book is different. It's built on stories, rituals, and practical steps that you can actually do—even if you're terrible at math, even if you hate numbers, even if the word "budget" makes you roll your eyes.

The promise is simple: financial happiness in 15 days or less. Not "riches," not "millions," but happiness. Peace. That warm sigh of relief when you realise you're not counting the days till payday. The quiet confidence of knowing that your money is working for you, not against you. That's the goal. And unlike most financial advice, this book isn't about abstract percentages or intimidating jargon. It's about the rhythm of your month. It's about walking with you day by day, like a friend who says, "Okay, it's Day 4, here's what we do now. Trust me."

Think of your month as a story you've been repeating forever. Act One: Payday joy. Act Two: mid-month surprises. Act Three: end-of-month regret. This book flips the script. By breaking the month into small, intentional steps, it teaches you how to rewrite your money story. Each chapter is a scene, each day a turning point. And together, they create a new narrative—one where you're in charge.

Why Money Feels So Emotional

Let's pause here and admit something: money isn't just about numbers. If it were, none of us would struggle. Addition and subtraction aren't that hard. What makes money complicated is that it's tied to our emotions. We don't spend ₹500 on a coffee because we're thirsty—we spend it because it makes us feel good, seen, and rewarded. We don't order food delivery at midnight because we're hungry—we order it because we're lonely, tired, or stressed. We don't swipe our card for that new phone because we need it—we do it because it makes us feel successful, updated, and part of the tribe. Every rupee we spend has a story behind it. And those stories are rarely logical. They're emotional. That's why pure mathematics never works in budgeting. You can't just divide your salary into neat percentages and expect obedience from your heart. You have to acknowledge the psychology of spending. You have to recognise your patterns, your triggers, and your weaknesses. This book doesn't shame you for them—it helps you work with them. Because once you see the money not as "numbers in an app" but as "pieces of your life energy," everything shifts.

Think about it this way: if you earn ₹45,000 a month and work 9 hours a day, you're making about ₹227 an hour. Every time you spend ₹900 on a casual dinner, you're trading four hours of your life. Sometimes it's worth it. Many times, it's not. The magic lies in pausing, noticing, and choosing with awareness.

What This Book Does Differently

There are thousands of finance books out there. Many of them are brilliant. Many of them sit unread on shelves because they feel too heavy, too complicated, too distant from everyday reality. What makes this one different? It's written for the salaried person who lives month to month, whose money comes in a predictable cycle, and yet vanishes unpredictably. It's structured not around lofty financial theories but around your actual calendar. Day 1, Day 2, Day 3. Payday, grocery day, bill day. The stuff you already live through. Instead of dumping information, it walks beside you.

It's also written with humour, because let's face it—money is stressful enough, without making it boring too. You'll find stories of midnight Swiggy binges of people who swear they'll save but end up with Amazon boxes stacked higher than their fridge, of couples who argue over EMIs and still buy another subscription they "absolutely need." Because real life is messy, and budgeting has to fit into that mess—not pretend it doesn't exist. Most importantly, this book is about design. You're not just "making do" with money; you're designing a life. Every rupee you assign becomes a brushstroke on the canvas of your month. And if you design it carefully, intentionally, with balance, you'll see something beautiful emerge: financial peace.

A Sneak Peek into the Journey

Without spoiling the chapters, let's take a little tour.

We start at the end of the previous month. Strange place to begin, right? But that's the secret. While everyone else waits for salary day, this book makes you sit down on Day 29, Day 30, Day 31, and plan. Not boring corporate-style planning, but honest, pen-on-paper clarity: what's coming in, what went out, what patterns repeat, what needs to change. It's like stretching before a run—no one loves it, but without it, you're limping by the halfway mark.

Then comes the thrill of payday. The rush of seeing money land in your account. Here, we learn to celebrate—but wisely. To treat ourselves without sabotaging the entire month. To spot payday sales without being trapped by them. To prioritise obligations, savings, and essentials before diving into wants. We build rituals that turn those first three days into a launchpad, not a disaster.

Next, we design the budget itself. Not a vague, abstract budget, but a living, breathing one. With categories that reflect real life: bills, essentials, fun, and one-time expenses. With checkpoints at Day 7, 15, and 25,you can course-correct before it's too late. With tricks like dividing your money weekly, so you never feel starved by Day 20.

Then we move into the daily battles: grocery planning like a French chef, turning boring necessities into opportunities for savings and joy. Financial housekeeping, where you declutter not just your home but your money life, clearing the cobwebs of overdue bills, forgotten subscriptions, and scattered receipts. Mid-month resets, where you pause, breathe, and realign instead of giving up. Challenges that gamify saving, making discipline feel fun.

And then we go deeper. Into the psychology of money. Into the red flags of budgeting—the traps that look harmless but derail everything. Into the habits of thought that make or break our savings. And finally, into charity. Yes, charity. Because money, when hoarded selfishly, loses its meaning. But when shared, it multiplies in ways you can't measure on a spreadsheet. Giving isn't just moral—it's financial karma.

By the time you close this book, you'll not just have a budget. You'll have a new relationship with money. One built on awareness, intention, and balance.

Why 15 Days Is Enough

You might wonder: why 15 days? Isn't financial discipline a lifelong pursuit? Of course it is. But the magic of 15 days is that it's long enough to build momentum and short enough to feel doable. You don't need a six-month course. You don't need to wait till the next financial year. In just half a month, you can establish the rituals, categories, and checkpoints that carry you forward.

Think of it like fitness. You don't need to train like an athlete for years to see change. Do a simple, consistent routine for two weeks, and you already feel stronger. Same with money. Two weeks of intentional actionscan reset the way you handle your salary forever.

A Word on Happiness

Notice the title says "financially happy," not "financially free" or "financially rich." Happiness is the goal. Freedom and richness may come later, but happiness is immediate. Happiness is sleeping without worrying about unpaid bills. Happiness is knowing your emergency fund is growing. Happiness is buying that ice cream without guilt because you budgeted for it. Happiness is the peace of mind that comes when money stops being a daily source of anxiety.

The Invitation

So, dear reader, here we are. Standing at the threshold of a journey that might change the way you live every month for the rest of your life. This prologue isn't a lecture—it's a handshake. An invitation. A whisper that says: "You can do this. You don't need to be a math genius. You don't need to give up joy. You just need to show up, day by day."

Chapter One is waiting. It begins not with the fireworks but with a quiet, deliberate act: pre-planning. The kind of act most people ignore. But those who embrace it never go back. Because when you start managing your money before it even arrives, you flip the script completely. You stop reacting to life and start designing it.

So, take a breath. Grab a pen if you like. Open your notes app if that's your style. And let's step into Day 29 together. Because financial happiness doesn't wait for the perfect salary, the perfect time, or the perfect miracle. It begins now. With you. With this page. With the choice to plan.

CHAPTER 1

PRE-PLANNING (DAYS 29 TO 31)

Laying the Groundwork Before Pay-Day

Purpose of the Chapter:

To help readers prepare mentally and practically before their salary arrives. This chapter encourages a habit of looking ahead, auditing the previous month, and mentally mapping out the next one. It sets the tone for financial clarity and control by treating the last few days of the month as a strategic pre-game.

What You'll Learn in This Chapter:

- Why pre-payday reflection is crucial to monthly success.
- How to audit the past month's budget performance.
- Planning recurring expenses and known financial obligations.
- Setting financial intentions and emotional goals.
- Building anticipation instead of anxiety before payday.
- Creating your "first three-day" playbook for the new month.

"A budget made before the salary arrives is ten times stronger than one made after it's spent."

CHAPTER I

PRE-PLANNING THE MONTH (DAYS 29 TO 31)

> *Every minute you spend on planning saves you ten minutes in execution. This gives you a 1000 per cent return on energy.*

Welcome to Day 29.

Most people don't start here. Most people jump straight to flashy investments, the latest finance apps, or hunting for side hustles. And don't get me wrong—those are great. But if you don't know how to manage what you already have, more money won't fix the problem. It might even make it worse. First, lay the foundation of your financial freedom. As Benjamin Franklin once said, "Failing to prepare is preparing to fail", so let us start with proper planning.

This is where we begin: the quiet, slightly boring but *essential* planning step. Not the kind that overwhelms you with complicated Excel sheets or forces you to live like a monk. No. This is practical, real-life pre-planning that fits into your current lifestyle—and slowly upgrades it. You don't need a finance degree.

You don't need to be great at math. You need three days at the end of every month to sit down with your money, look it in the eye, and say, "Let's figure this out together."

Let's start with what you actually earn.

That big number on your offer letter? That's your **CTC**—Cost to the Company. It includes everything: your salary, bonuses, benefits, and often, stuff you never see in cash (like the employer's share of Provident Fund). So, while your CTC might say ₹7,00,000 per year, your actual **take-home pay**—the amount that lands in your bank—is usually much less. Let's say after taxes and deductions, you get ₹45,000/month. That's your **net salary**. That's the number that matters. That's what you budget with.

Take 10 minutes right now. Open your salary slip or bank app. What was your actual income last month? Write that down. That's your real number. Step one, done.

If you're salaried, taxes are usually already taken out, usually in the last four months or six months of the financial year. But don't skip this step. Understanding how much you're taxed—and *why*—helps you make better financial decisions. Check your salary slip. Look for:

- **TDS** (Tax Deducted at Source)
- **Professional Tax**
- **Employee Provident Fund (EPF)**

If you're a freelancer or run a business, this is even more crucial. Track all your income and consult a CA (Chartered Accountant) or use a tax calculator. Because surprise tax deductions are no fun.

And remember tax planning isn't just about paying less. It's about being prepared. That peace of mind? Totally worth it.

> ***Pro-tip**: If you know at what slab you are taxed, deduct that amount from your monthly salary in small instalments and put it in a recurring deposit. This way, the income tax deduction in the last four months of the year won't put you in a crunch at the same time you can earn interest on your deposit.*

This next step is really powerful. Take a printout of your salary slip and your last month's bank statement in full detail. Yes, really—**print them**. The bank statement should contain all narrations, credits, debits and remaining balance columns. Get a highlighter. Get messy.

Highlight:

- Recurring expenses (Netflix, rent, etc.)
- Random spends (late-night Swiggy and Zomato, impulsive Amazon buys)
- Deductions you don't fully understand (Google them!)

When you see your financial life on paper, it *hits different*ly. It becomes real. Tangible. Sometimes clarity doesn't come from another app. It comes from good old paper and pen. When you see how much you spend on unjustified emotional impulses, your determination gets stronger, and you want more than ever to become financially disciplined. You start to see a pattern.

Patterns hide in plain sight. Let's find them.

Do this:

- Look at your debit column
- Spot the things that keep showing up.

Swiggy every Friday? Cab or Bike Taxi every morning? Phone recharge three times a month?

These repeated spends are your low-hanging fruit. Fix one or two, and you'll instantly free up money. Maybe a weekly meal plan cuts your Swiggy bill in half. Maybe a monthly recharge saves you ₹100. Maybe carpooling slashes your fuel bill.

Awareness is power.

The next step is to track your expenses. Now you're getting into the deep stuff. You can't manage what you don't measure. Tracking your expenses isn't as boring as it sounds. You don't need fancy tools. Try to keep a daily journal. A small notebook, or you can even note this on your WhatsApp. Or just pick one app that fits your vibe.

Try Google Sheets, Walnut, Money Manager, Axio or Notion templates or any such app you like.

I know this is hard, but try to do this. This journal isn't about being poetic. It's about **emotional clarity**. Here's what to jot down:

- What did I spend on today?
- Why did I spend it?
- How did I feel after?

That's it. Three small questions. Over time, patterns emerge.

Maybe you shop when you're stressed. Maybe food delivery spikes every time work gets overwhelming. Maybe weekends equal mindless swiping. This isn't about judgment. It's about **recognition**. When you see the "why" behind your habits, you get the power to change them. Don't overthink it. The tool is less important than the **habit**. Spend 5 minutes every evening noting down what you spent and on what. You'll be shocked at how just writing it down changes your behaviour. And no, you don't need to become an accountant. You just need to be *aware*. You can't fix what you don't understand.

Money isn't just a number—it's a piece of your time, energy, and effort.

Let's break it down: if you earn ₹45,000/month, and work 9 hours a day, 22 days a month, you're earning ₹227/hour. Every ₹227 you spend is *one hour of your life*.

So, the next time you feel the itch to buy something impulsively—maybe a ₹900 food delivery—pause and ask, "Is this worth four hours of my work?" Sometimes the answer is yes (you had a long week, treat yourself). But often, just that moment of awareness will change your decision. This isn't about guilt. It's about consciousness. When you value your time, you value your money. And that shift changes everything.

Try to recognise emotional spending areas. We all have our triggers. Some people eat when they're upset. Some shop when they're bored. Some swipe their card when they're lonely. And companies *know this*. That's why you see food ads late at night and sales right after payday.

Your job is to understand your patterns. When do you spend most impulsively? What emotion usually comes before? Once you know the trigger, you can change the response. Sad? Instead of scrolling through Amazon, call a friend. Bored? Instead of food delivery, go for a walk, or maybe play a game or watch a movie.

Money habits are *emotional* habits. Let's handle them with care.

The next step is to categorise your expenses. Here's where most people go wrong. They see ₹45,000 and think they can spend it however they like, with a little control. But that control rarely comes into action. Until—suddenly—it's Day 20, and they're wondering where it all went. Human beings are emotional creatures by design. No matter how much we think about control, we will finally give in to our temptations.

The fix? Break your expenses into categories. Draw this table on paper and fill in the boxes with the expense categories. Take the help of your bank statement you took a print of earlier.

SPEND CATEGORIES	
Bills/EMIs: (Home EMI, Phone EMI, electric bill, water bill, etc.)	Essentials:(Grocery, Medicines, Wi-Fi, Insurance, Petrol, etc.)
Fun: (Food orders, Movies, Eating out, Shopping, etc.)	Impulsive Expenses: (Amazon orders, New Subscriptions, Late-night orders, Parties, etc.)

Write them down. Assign a ballpark figure to each. Even a rough plan is better than no plan. See where your money is going at the end of the month. When you give every rupee a "job," your money works *for* you—not against you.

At the end, check this: **how much is left for savings?** Are you satisfied with this amount? If not, things need to change. Always remember this rule,

1. **Savings ⇔ Debt**
2. **Fun ⇔ Savings**
3. **Big Purchases ⇔ Essentials**

Next, Decide How Much You're Comfortable Saving (Use the 50-30-20 Rule). We will discuss this method in detail in the next chapter.

Let's keep this simple:

50% of your salary → *Needs*

30% → *Wants*

20% → *Savings*

For a ₹45,000 net salary:

- ₹22,500 = Essentials
- ₹13,500 = Lifestyle (dining, shopping, fun stuff)
- ₹9,000 = Savings

This isn't a law—it's a starting point. If it feels too tight, tweak it. Maybe do 60-30-10 for now, and work your way up. The goal isn't perfection. It's *consistency*. The only thing worse than saving too little is saving nothing at all.

There is one thing more important than savings: an emergency fund. Before you invest or lock away your savings, create an **emergency fund**. This fund will be your personal "oops" fund. A backup. Your cushion against life's little surprises—like a sudden medical bill, your bike breaking down, or something more serious like losing your job. Start small. Even ₹1,000/month is in progress. Park it in a separate account—not the one linked to UPI or your debit card. Out of sight equals out of spend. Ideally, there should be enough funds to last you six months without income, but you can start with three. Your future self, will *hug you* when something goes wrong and you're like, "Ah. I've got this."

Next, you need to plan your payment dates. Note down what fixed expenses are going out and on which dates. Money management isn't just about *how much* you spend—it's about *when* you spend it.

List down fixed expense amounts and dates:

- **Rent due** (₹10000)
- **EMIs** (₹5000)
- **SIPs** (₹3000)
- **Credit card bill** (₹5000)
- **Utility payments** (₹5000)
- **Subscriptions** (₹10000)

Now, set reminders. Google Calendar. Phone alarms. Sticky notes. Whatever works for you. It is even better to automate the payments when possible. Because late fees are just money lost to forgetfulness. Let's not do that anymore.

Now, since you have tracked all your fixed expenses, you have a clear idea about the money you have at hand to spend during this month. The next thing to do is, you have to set spending limits. Here's a small trick that changes everything: think weekly, not monthly. Let's say you've allocated ₹13,500 for your "wants" (food, movies, shopping, etc.). That sounds fine in theory—but what often happens? You blow half of it in the first week, and then spend the rest of the month guilt-tripping yourself.

Instead, divide that ₹13,500 into 4 weekly chunks. That's about ₹3,375/week. Now, you've got a real-time budget. If you go over one week, dial it down the next. Simple. This creates built-in checkpoints. You stay aware. You stay in control. Also, it makes your money *last*. And that's a sweet, underrated feeling.

> ***Pro-tip****: Divide the money in hand by 4.3, which will give you the amount you are allowed to spend in a week. Why 4.3 and not 4, you ask? That is because some months have 31 days instead of 30.*

You still have a few tasks left to finish before you can get a clear picture of the month to come. What money will you have and what money you are allowed to spend? Start from the current month and go forward. And before you move forward, take a few minutes to look back. Be honest. Be gentle. Ask:

- Did I overspend anywhere?
- Did I miss any due dates?
- Did I go off-plan with my budget?

Note down *what* went wrong—and *why*. Did a friend's wedding throw off your budget? Did you forget to track expenses mid-month? Did stress lead to impulse shopping? Whatever it is, write it without guilt. This isn't about beating yourself up. It's about building a smarter you. **The only mistake is the one we keep repeating.** Time to open your bank statement's printout and scroll through your last month's transactions. Identify the top three spending areas. For most people, it's:

- Food delivery
- Cabs or fuel
- Online shopping

Now ask:

- Was it worth it?
- Would I do it again?
- What would I change?

If you find yourself saying, "Well... maybe not," that's your opportunity. Justify every spend. Use that wisdom in the coming month. Whenever you feel like spending a rupee, you will remember the fact that you had marked it "UNJUSTIFIED SPEND" the previous month and that kick will hit you in the back of your head the next time you start entering that UPI pin.

You don't need to cut it out completely. Just *trim the excess.* Small tweaks → big savings.

Also, if these "unexpected" expenses happen often... maybe they're not that unexpected.

Budgeting is about **anticipating the real world**. If something happens every 2–3 months, start planning for it monthly. That way, when it does come, it doesn't throw you off.

Now, let's clean the slate.

Make a quick list of your overdues:

- Credit card dues?
- Missed loan EMIs?
- Utility bills?
- That ₹500 you owe a friend?

Write it all down. Clear it if you can. If not, don't feel bad about it. You are just beginning this journey. Write down the amounts and due dates in a journal. You will use this data in the next month's budget and try to clear it slowly from your designed financial plan. Overdues are emotional baggage. They sit in the back of your mind, draining mental energy. Starting a new month with unpaid bills is like entering a race with a backpack full of rocks. Let's drop the load, or at least plan to keep dropping each stone at a time.

Now, some expenses are necessary and can be anticipated and planned. The next thing you will do is make a list of all the one-time expenses in a year. Like mom's birthday, when you buy a gift for her or maybe your anniversary, when you go out for a lavish dinner.

Got plans for next month?

- Cousin's wedding?

- Friend's birthday?
- Laptop repair?
- Annual insurance?

These are **predictable surprises**. The kind that shows up often and ruins a good budget. List them now. Set aside a small amount for each. You need to know the amounts you are comfortable spending on each event, which will make your budget design easier.

Planning is how you enjoy life *without* debt, guilt, or panic.

Now, since all preparation is almost done. You need that rocket fuel to keep that rocket rising. And your rocket fuel (motivation) will be a goal. A small achievable goal, and I repeat, **achievable**, that will give you that much-needed push to stay within your defined limits every time.

Set a goal for next month.:

- "I'll save ₹5,000 for my buffer fund."
- "I'll reduce Swiggy orders from 10 to 3."
- "I'll use public transport twice a week instead of cabs."
- "I will add ₹4000 to my new car downpayment fund"

And so on. The sky is the limit. Clear goals equal clear action. Keep it small. Keep it doable. Big changes are built from tiny consistent wins.

Lastly, let's not forget the unsung hero of financial peace: **organisation**. Create at least three physical files at home. Name your files clearly and keep them within reach. At least make these 3 files.

1. Bills
2. Rent Receipts/ Home Loan EMI
3. Insurance Payments

and make other files according to your discretion. Organised finances reduce stress. You'll never fumble during tax season or wonder if that EMI went through. I have been there where I have to run a search through my whole inbox to find that receipt, I have to add to my tax deduction or have to claim a warranty using that purchase bill. Plus, you'll feel *like a boss.* And you are one.

Most people think budgeting is about restriction. About saying no to fun. But budgeting is about saying yes—on your terms. When you pre-plan your money, you choose where it goes. That's real freedom. Planning isn't boring—it's your blueprint for the life you want. Some months you'll feel like a genius. Others, not so much.

What matters is:

- Show up every month.
- Review without judgment.
- Adjust without drama.
- Keep going.

Consistency beats intensity. And as life changes, so should your plan. You're not building a rigid system. You're building a flexible foundation.

So instead of waiting for the next raise or crisis. You're starting now. With what you have. Where you are. So, let's do this. Open your notes. Make your categories. Pull out your salary slip and bank statement. Do your 3-day review. Because when you plan your money, you don't just survive the month—you start designing a life you love.

☑ Key Takeaways From This Chapter

- Understand your **real income** (Net Salary).
- Deduct **taxes** according to your slab.
- Print your salary slip + bank statement.
- Highlight **recurring, random, unnecessary** spends.
- Track daily expenses in a **journal/app**.
- Categorise into **Essentials, Wants, Impulses.**
- Apply the **50-30-20 Rule** (or a modified version).
- Start building an **Emergency Fund.**
- List all **fixed expenses** and due dates.
- Set **weekly spending limits.**
- Write down and plan to clear **overdues.**
- Anticipate **predictable surprises.**
- Set a **clear, achievable monthly goal.**
- Organise documents into **files.**

Exercises for You

1. Take your last month's bank statement. Highlight impulsive spending in red. Stick it on your study wall.
2. Draw a **pie chart** of your expenses: Essentials, Wants, Savings, Impulses. Colour it.

3. On a blank sheet, write your income. Break it into **weekly boxes**. Cross out spends as you go.
4. Role-play with a friend: justify a ₹2000 spend. Then switch sides and argue against it.
5. Use **envelopes or jars** labelled Essentials, Wants, Savings. Put real cash or mock notes to simulate budgeting.

CHAPTER 2

PAY DAY PLANNING (DAY 1)

Turning Your Salary into a Strategy

Purpose of the Chapter:

To show readers how to handle their salary during the first three days with structure and clarity. Rather than impulsively spending or paying bills randomly, this chapter walks through a step-by-step process to allocate, prioritise, and protect income from day one.

What You'll Learn in This Chapter:

- How to emotionally reset on payday to avoid impulsive decisions
- Building a "Salary Split System" to allocate money by purpose
- The importance of fixed commitments vs. flexible spending
- Creating a financial rhythm and rituals every payday
- How to automate, organise, and stay accountable

"What you do in the first 3 days determines how the next 27 days will feel."

CHAPTER II

PAY DAY PLANNING (DAY 1)

> *The best way to make your salary last is to plan before it starts flying out the door.*

Welcome to Day 1.

It's Pay Day! The glorious day when your hard work translates into numbers on your bank screen. It's that magical notification that hits your phone—*"₹50,000 credited to your salary account."* Ah, the dopamine rush! It's like your bank app is throwing you a mini-party. The one day that makes every Monday, every deadline, and every 9 AM Teams call feel worth it.

You got the notification, sure. But slow down—don't assume everything is perfect. The immediate next step is to verify your salary. Always verify:

- Was the correct amount deposited?
- Were bonuses, incentives, or reimbursements included?
- Any surprising deductions?
- Did your variable pay come through?

It's not about doubting your employer—it's about being *aware*. Treat it like checking the specs of your favourite car or motorcycle. Understand every bit, every deduction in your salary. If you are unsure about anything, ask your HR or someone from your friends and family who can clear the doubts for you. You wouldn't want a surprise ingredient (or a missing one), right?

Also, tracking your salary consistently helps spot patterns:

- Are reimbursements or variables delayed often?
- Are deductions increasing?
- Did your TDS go up?

When you're informed, you're empowered. You can make better decisions, plan smarter, and avoid nasty surprises later.

> ***Pro-tip:*** *Create a simple Excel sheet or use a notes app to log your salary details every month. Over time, you'll spot patterns instantly.*

Now, before anything else, first treat yourself, you deserve to celebrate. You've pushed through deadlines, survived the Monday blues, and maybe even endured the wrath of a tough boss or a painfully long commute. Go ahead—acknowledge your effort. But celebrate wisely, and avoid the "Pay Day Splurge". Instead of going on an impulsive shopping spree or booking a luxury dinner right away, set a mini "celebration budget" Pick a range—₹500 to ₹1000. That's your guilt-free treat budget. It can be a new shirt, pizza night, or even that long-awaited Kindle e-book. The key is this: you're rewarding yourself *without sabotaging your month.* Here's why this matters. If your payday starts with chaos—random orders, unplanned spending, emotional purchases (which most people do for the first 3 days)—you've already lost the game. But if it starts with intention and proper planning, even the fun feels more fulfilling.

> ***Pro-tip:*** *Pre-decide your treat before payday. It avoids impulsive splurges because you've already chosen something meaningful.*

Now it's time to reflect on your rocket fuel. I hope you remember this from our previous chapter. The one thing that will keep you on track this month. So, before your fingers go wild tapping away at your UPI app, take a moment. Just 5 minutes. Breathe. Sit down. Ask yourself this question:

What is my financial goal this month?

This reflection is your shield against impulse. It switches your brain from *spender* to *strategist*. You start seeing your money not as "something to use," but as "something to guide."

Example:

- Last month, maybe you overspent on food delivery. So, this month, your goal could be to "cook 5 meals a week."
- Or maybe you overspent on transport, so you will commute on public transport 4 times a week.
- Or maybe you will send ₹5000 more to your emergency fund.

This mini self-check brings clarity. Do it every payday morning like a ritual, and you'll start mastering your money—not the other way around.

Now, before you start budgeting, it's time for a scavenger hunt. One of the coolest perks of living in the digital age? Payday sales. E-commerce platforms, food delivery apps, clothing brands—even banks and credit card companies—love to tempt us with "Pay Day Offers" during the first week of the month. And it makes total sense: they know that's when most people get paid. Note this down in a notebook, you are going to use these sales to buy your essentials like groceries and other wish list items. Mark the days when they end, for example, a sale on SmartBazar might end on the 5th of the month and set a reminder the day before. Set the reminder on your Google calendar or phone alarm, whatever works for you.

Here's what you might see: Amazon/Flipkart running flash sales from the 1st to the 5th of every month. Zepto/Blinkit is offering 20% off on first-week orders. Clothing brands are throwing in extra discounts on already discounted items. Banks or credit cards offering 10% instant cashback on specific days.

Sounds tempting, right? It can be—if you're smart about it.

Use these sales *only* if:

- You already planned to buy that item (e.g., a kitchen appliance, a budgeted outfit for a wedding, or a pair of running shoes you've needed for a while).
- The discount fits within your budget.
- You aren't swiping a credit card you can't repay later.

Don't fall for: "It's on sale, so I should buy it" logic or buying things just because the deal seems good. Remember, a good deal is only good if you actually need it. Otherwise, it's just money leaving your account in disguise.

> ***Pro-tip***: *Set a "wishlist" throughout the month. When the payday sales roll in, check if anything from your list is on discount. If yes—and if it fits your budget—you score both the item and the deal. Win-win!*

After this and before you start budgeting, you need to prioritise your expenses. Think of your income like a delicious buffet. If you go straight for the desserts, you might miss the nutritious stuff your body (and budget) really needs. So, what should be served first on your financial plate? Follow the hierarchy below. And never break this hierarchy.

Priority 1. Fixed Obligations – Non-Negotiables First

These are the "must-pays." They don't care if you had fun or not—they're due every month without fail.

Examples:

- Rent or home loan EMI
- Utility bills (electricity, Wi-Fi, gas, phone)
- Loan EMIs (personal, car, education)
- Credit card bills

Why first? These expenses usually have fixed due dates and missing them can lead to penalties, late fees, or worse—damage to your credit score. Plus, it clears your head knowing the basics are covered. We have already talked about the importance of auto-debiting these expenses, but always cross-check the deduction amounts and dates. And keep a sufficient balance in your account.

Priority 2. Savings & Investments – Pay Yourself Next

This might surprise you. Most people save *after* they spend. But the golden rule of financial success is to save first and spend later. Treat your savings like a bill—something you *must* pay every month. Split this section into:

- Emergency fund top-up (if used last month)
- SIPs (Systematic Investment Plans)
- Recurring deposits
- Digital gold or retirement savings
- Tax-saving instruments (ELSS, PPF, NPS)

If you have not started investing in all these instruments, don't worry. Even saving ₹1000 is a start. The key is to build the habit. Move this amount to a separate account or investment platform on Day 1. The earlier it's out of reach, the safer it is.

Priority 3. Essentials – Everyday Living Costs

Next, it's time to budget for your daily living expenses.

This includes:

- Groceries
- Petrol/diesel
- Daily travel or commute costs
- Toiletries and household needs
- Mobile/data recharge
- Medicines

Create a realistic budget based on your previous months. Essentials often vary, but keeping a rough range (e.g., ₹5000–₹8000 for an individual) helps.

> ***Pro-tip**: If you live with family, this section might be shared. Clarify who covers what.*

Priority 4. Wants & Discretionary Expenses – The Fun Stuff

Once the important stuff is handled, we get to the fun part—but with a plan! This might include dining out, ordering food, movies and subscriptions, shopping, and impulse buys (yes, we all have them). Set a "wants" budget—maybe ₹4000 or ₹5000. Transfer it to a UPI wallet or use a prepaid card.

> ***Pro-tip**: Once it's gone, it's gone. No topping it up mid-month. This keeps your budget healthy and spending guilt-free.*

Bonus Priority: Buffer for Unexpected Expenses

Even with the best planning, surprises happen like bike repairs, sudden travel, gifts or last-minute expenses. Set aside ₹1000–₹2000 as a mini buffer. If not used, it can roll into savings next month.

Here's a sample allocation from a ₹50,000 monthly salary:

Priority	Category	Amount
Fixed Obligations	Rent + EMIs + Bills	₹ 18,000
Savings/ Investments	SIPs + Emergency + PPF	₹ 10,000

Essentials	Groceries + Transport	₹ 7,000
Wants	Dining + Shopping + Fun	₹ 5,000
Buffer	Miscellaneous/ Unexpected	₹ 2,000
Leftover	To roll over or reassign	₹ 8,000

This is flexible! You can adjust based on goals, upcoming events, or financial situations—but the priority sequence stays the same. And remember, never break this order of priority.

Now, before you start allocating funds to different sections. Use a "Budget Rule" that works for you (50-30-20 or Your Variant). Here's a classic rule that works for most people: the 50-30-20 Rule.

- 50% for Needs – rent, groceries, transport
- 30% for Wants – shopping, entertainment, eating out
- 20% for Savings/Investments – for your future

Example on ₹50,000 income:

- Needs: ₹25,000
- Wants: ₹15,000
- Savings: ₹10,000

But let's be real—life isn't a math equation. Some months your rent is higher. Some months there's a wedding or festival. So, treat this rule as a starting point, not a strict cage. Customise your ratio according to your needs. Maybe this month you aim for

40-30-30 because you want to invest more. Or maybe it's 60-20-20 because of a medical bill. Flex it—but never skip the savings.

> ***Pro-tip:*** *Experiment with different rules (like 60-20-20 or 40-30-30) until you find one that fits your lifestyle. Flexibility is key.*

But remember this, too. Always keep your reserve fuel tank full. If you used your emergency fund last month, congratulations. It did exactly what it was meant to do. Maybe your bike broke down, your pet needed a vet visit, or there was a family emergency. Now, it's time to top it back up.

The ideal emergency fund size is 6 months of essential expenses, but as I said you can start with 3 months if you like and slowly let it grow to 6 months. But top-up whenever necessary. If your monthly essentials are ₹25,000, aim for ₹50,000–₹75,000 in your emergency fund. That may sound huge, but it's okay to build slowly. Even putting ₹2000 this month is a win.

Where to park it? Avoid parking emergency money in FDs with penalties or risky instruments like stocks. Investing your emergency fund in a liquid mutual fund is one of the smartest moves you can make if you want your money to stay safe, grow modestly, and remain accessible when you need it most. Unlike keeping it in a regular savings account where it earns minimal interest, a liquid mutual fund typically offers better returns—anywhere between 3.5% to 6% annually—without exposing you to high risk. These funds invest in short-term debt instruments like treasury bills and commercial papers, which makes them relatively stable and low-volatility. The biggest advantage? You can usually withdraw your money within 24 hours, without any penalty, which makes it nearly as accessible as a bank account. This is especially important for emergencies, where time is often of the essence. At the same time, keeping your emergency fund slightly "out of sight" in a separate investment helps prevent unnecessary spending. You're less likely to dip into it for non-urgent reasons if it's not sitting idle in your main account. It's like creating a financial speed bump—you can still get to the money, but you'll think twice before touching it. Over time, even small monthly top-ups into a liquid fund can grow into a comforting financial cushion that gives you both peace of mind and practical support.

You also need to include a debt repayment plan in your budget. Loans can be overwhelming, but planning makes them manageable.

Use either:

A) **Avalanche Method**: The Avalanche Method is all about paying less interest over time. You tackle the debt with the highest interest rate first, then work your way down. It may take longer to get your first win, but you'll save more money in the long run.

Example:

- Credit Card A: ₹5,000 at 18%
- Personal Loan: ₹20,000 at 14%
- Credit Card B: ₹10,000 at 22%

With the Avalanche Method, you'd attack Credit Card B first—because 22% interest is burning through your wallet the fastest. You pay minimums on the other two while throwing everything extra at Card B. Once that's paid off, you move to Credit Card A, then the Personal Loan. Why use it? Because mathematically, it's the most efficient. You'll pay less interest overall and become debt-free faster *in total*, even if the early wins are slower.

B) **Snowball Method**: Pay off the smallest loan first for motivation. The Snowball Method focuses on momentum and motivation. You pay off your smallest debt first, regardless of the interest rate. Once that's gone, you move on to the next smallest one, and so on. Like a snowball rolling downhill, your confidence (and extra money) builds as each debt disappears.

Same Example:

- Let's say you have these debts:
- Credit Card A: ₹5,000 at 18% interest
- Personal Loan: ₹20,000 at 14% interest
- Credit Card B: ₹10,000 at 22% interest

With the Snowball Method, you'd pay off Credit Card A first—because it has the smallest balance—even though it doesn't have the highest interest. You pay minimums on the other two and throw any extra money at Card A. Once that's cleared, you move to Credit Card B, then finally the Personal Loan. Why use it? Because seeing quick wins keeps you motivated. It's emotionally satisfying to cross debts off your list—even if it's not the most mathematically "optimal" path.

> ***Pro-tip:*** *Use a debt calculator app to simulate repayment timelines. It helps visualise which method (Avalanche vs Snowball) works best for you.*

Next, anticipate big expenses this month and include them in your budget. Avoid budget bombs mid-month. Sit with your calendar and ask:

- Are there birthdays, weddings, or travel this month?
- Is car/bike insurance due?
- Any doctor visits or school fees?

Estimate the costs now. Allocate funds. If it's big, break it down into parts and start a mini-sinking fund. Planning for these *now* keeps you from panic-spending later.

Use 3 Accounts for Maximum Simplicity

Here's a structure that changes everything:

1. **Bills Account** – for rent, EMIs, auto-debits
2. **Daily Use Account** – for groceries, fuel, etc.
3. **Savings/Investment Account** – untouched except for growth

Using three separate bank accounts for managing your salary isn't just a finance hack—it's a mindset shift. It brings structure, clarity, and control to your money. Most of us keep everything in one account, and that's where the chaos starts. You see a big number right after payday and think, *"I'm rich!"*—but two weeks later, you're wondering where it all went. Splitting your salary into three dedicated accounts helps you break that cycle.

Here's why it works so well. One account is your Bills Account. This is for all your fixed, non-negotiable expenses like rent, EMIs, utilities, and subscriptions. The second one is your Essentials/Daily Use Account, which you'll use for groceries, transport, eating out, and general life expenses. And the third is your Savings/Investment Account—where you pay your future self, first ,before spending a rupee on anything else. This account is sacred. You don't touch it unless it's for investing or saving toward a goal.

This setup creates natural boundaries. You don't have to constantly calculate how much is left for spending. You just check your daily-use account and know exactly what you can afford. It also reduces the temptation to dip into savings when things get tight. In short, three accounts give you a built-in system that's simple, stress-free, and smart.

Even better? Use digital wallets for daily spending to isolate your fun money. Spending from digital wallets often includes bonuses and extra cashback.

Budget your pocket money (Yes, Even Adults Need This!). Give yourself an allowance. Seriously. It may sound silly, but setting a personal "pocket money" limit keeps your budget safe.

Example:

- ₹4000 for the month = ₹1000/week for personal spending.

- This covers coffee dates, random purchases, snacks, and impulse buys.

When you limit your fun money, you:

- Spend guilt-free (within limits)
- Avoid tapping into savings
- Build self-control like a boss

Now, your preparation has almost come to an end. Next, you will get your hands dirty and start drawing your budget sheet in Excel. But before that, identify red flag spending zones. Everyone has a money trap. Yours could be food delivery apps, late-night Amazon browsing, peer-pressure outings or trendy gadgets. Be honest with yourself. Track where you overspend most, and set limits or blockers. Take drastic steps, for example, uninstall Zomato temporarily, keep the UPI app locked at night, and avoid mall browsing when bored.

Last but not least, involve your family. If you're not managing finances solo, involve your people. Sit with your spouse, parents, or flatmates and share the budget, talk about your plans, divide responsibilities or set savings goals together. Two is always better than one. Money silence creates confusion. Money talks create collaboration. And if you're living at home or sharing expenses, this becomes even more important.

Think of Day 1 to Day 3 as your monthly launchpad. The quality of these 3 days shapes your next 27. Anyone can earn money. But building a plan—that's what creates financial peace. Every time your salary arrives, it gives you two choices: either to let it flow out mindlessly or guide it with purpose. Choose the second. Do it month after month. And before you know it, you'll look back and smile at how far you've come.

☑ Key Takeaways From This Chapter

- Check for deductions, bonuses, or anomalies.
- Reward yourself, but keep it within your ₹500–₹1000 'treat budget.'
- Spend 5 minutes setting your financial focus for the month.
- Track first-week sales and use them for planned purchases only.
- Follow the golden order: Obligations → Savings → Essentials → Wants → Buffer.
- Test the 50-30-20 rule or create your own version.
- Keep it at 3–6 months of essentials. Refill if used.
- Use Avalanche (save on interest) or Snowball (quick wins).
- Birthdays, weddings, EMIs, or insurance renewals—budget them early.
- Separate bills, daily use, and savings/investments.
- Fix a weekly allowance for guilt-free spending.
- Share, align, and collaborate on money goals.

Exercises for You

1. Take a sheet of paper and draw three columns titled: Obligations, Savings, Essentials. Write down your expected amounts for each this month.
2. Open your UPI or banking app and physically transfer ₹500–₹1000 into a 'treat' wallet. Feel the action of separating it.
3. Create a mini 'debt ladder' with sticky notes on a wall – each note represents a loan. Remove one when you clear it. The physical act builds momentum.
4. Write your financial goal for the month on a post-it and stick it on your fridge or desk. Look at it daily.
5. Use coins or tokens to simulate your budget allocations on a table. Physically move them between categories to see where money flows.

CHAPTER 3

DESIGNING A DETAILED BUDGET (DAYS 2 AND 3)

Creating a Budget That Works for Your Real Life

Purpose of the Chapter:

To walk readers through the actual process of building a budget that reflects not just logic, but personality, lifestyle, priorities, and goals. This chapter helps design a budget you can actually live with—not just admire on paper.

What You'll Learn in This Chapter:

- The anatomy of a realistic, effective monthly budget
- Budgeting for needs, wants, goals, and buffers
- Using historical spending to forecast future needs
- Including mental health, lifestyle, and social life in your plan
- Building in flexibility, fun, and future planning

"Your budget should not feel like a cage—it should feel like a compass."

CHAPTER III

DESIGNING YOUR DETAILED BUDGET (DAYS 2 & 3)

"

Design can be art. Design is so simple, that's why it's so complicated.

Welcome to Day 2 and Day 3—arguably the heart of your monthly financial journey! After the rush of Pay Day fades, now comes the crucial step: giving every rupee a home, a purpose, and a plan. If Day 1 was the party, Days 2 and 3 are about picking up the pen, rolling up your sleeves, and taking charge. Don't worry—this doesn't mean endless spreadsheets and complicated charts. Budgeting can be as simple or detailed as you want it to be, as long as it makes sense to you and keeps your finances in check.

Pro-tip: *Budgeting isn't about restriction—it's about freedom. The more control you have, the more confident you feel when spending.*

Let's take a friendly stroll through the art of designing your personal budget, step by step. Think of your budget as a blueprint for your month. It's not just about controlling your spending—it's about consciously choosing where your money goes. It's your plan for comfort, savings, peace of mind, and fun. You've worked hard for your income, so now it's time to ensure every rupee works just as hard for you. A well-crafted budget helps prevent the mid-month panic, the end-of-month struggle, and the guilt of splurging without a safety net. Designing a budget is not restrictive—it's empowering.

A bad budget doesn't just ruin one month—it creates a domino effect that can throw off your entire financial stability for months to come. When your budget is unrealistic, vague, or overly optimistic, it often leads to overspending or missing key expenses. Let's say you underestimate your electricity bill or forget to factor in an annual insurance premium—suddenly, you're dipping into savings or swiping a credit card to cover the gap. This pushes your next month's income toward repaying that overspend instead of funding your current needs or goals. Slowly, the debt snowballs, savings shrink, and you're constantly playing catch-up. Worse, the emotional toll adds up—stress, anxiety, and guilt creep in, making it harder to stick to any plan. People often respond by abandoning budgeting altogether, thinking it doesn't work, when in fact, it was just poorly designed. Without a solid, realistic budget, there's no structure to guide your decisions and financial goals—like saving for emergencies, investing, or planning big purchases—get sidelined. Month after month, this cycle repeats, leading to a situation where you're always behind, reacting to money problems instead of controlling them. That's why a thoughtful, well-planned budget isn't just helpful—it's essential for long-term peace of mind.

Let's keep this simple. Start by taking out your notebook or opening Excel on your laptop—whatever you're comfortable with. Now list your total income for the month. That's your starting point. When you clearly list every rupee coming in—whether it's your salary, freelance payments, rental income, interest from savings, or side hustle earnings—you get a complete picture of what you're actually working with. This clarity helps you make realistic spending decisions, avoid overestimating your financial capacity, and plan your expenses accordingly.

Most people budget only based on their main income, forgetting small but regular earnings like cashback rewards, weekend tutoring, or dividend payouts. These might seem minor, but when added up, they can strengthen your financial plan or support savings goals. On the flip side, not accounting for irregular or seasonal income can make your budget feel tight or unpredictable. Documenting every income stream also helps you track your progress over time. Are your side gigs growing? Are your investments beginning to pay off? Writing it all down shows you trends and opportunities you might otherwise miss. It's like laying the foundation of a house—when the base is solid, everything built on top stands stronger. In short, noting down all your income is the first smart move toward financial control and peace of mind.

Below, I have given a list of the most common sources of income an individual tends to have. Put the figures that apply to you.

Income	Amount (₹)
1. Salary	
2. Incentives	
3. Conveyance	
4. Other variables	
5. Interest Income	
6. Professional Income	
7. Rental Income	
8. Dividend Income	
9. Capital Gains	
10. Government Schemes	
11. Freelancing	
12. Gifts	
13. Owed Money	
14. Royalties	
15. Referral/Cashbacks	
16. Tuition Income	
17. Other sources	
18. Rollover from previous month.	
19. Total	

Next, list all your known expenses—things like rent, groceries, school fees, transport, EMIs, mobile bills, subscriptions, and so on. Do not worry about categorising them in order.

We will talk about that later in this chapter. For now, try to remember as many expenses as you can and list them down on paper. Don't forget occasional expenses—like birthdays, repairs, or an upcoming family function. If you plan for them, they won't catch you off guard.

Once everything is listed, organise them into clear categories. This is where things start to take shape. Take a pen and paper and start getting dirty. Creating categories helps you organise your money with clarity. Categorising your expenses is a powerful way to take control of your finances, and doing it in a clear, structured manner makes budgeting much easier and more effective. Breaking your spending into categories like Bills, Savings, Essentials, Fun Money, and One-Time Expenses help you understand where your money is going, spot areas of overspending, and make intentional choices with your income. Do remember that following the same hierarchy is inevitable. Bills->Savings->Essentials->Fun Money. The last category, i.e. "One-Time Expenses", is an occasional category which might not show up every month, so that will not come under our hierarchy system, but it is important nonetheless.

Bills include recurring, non-negotiable payments like rent, electricity, phone, internet, and EMIs. These are your fixed responsibilities, and they should be prioritised first in your budget so nothing important gets missed.

Savings are your investment in the future—whether it's for an emergency fund, a big purchase, retirement, or financial freedom. Treat this like a non-negotiable bill to yourself. By assigning a clear portion of your income to savings, you ensure steady progress toward your long-term goals.

Essentials cover your day-to-day living expenses like groceries, transport, and basic healthcare. These are flexible but necessary, and setting a specific limit helps avoid overspending.

Fun Money is what keeps life enjoyable—dining out, hobbies, entertainment, shopping, etc. Allocating a fixed amount guilt-free keeps you from feeling restricted and actually helps you stick to your budget.

One-time expenses like gifts, repairs, or festival shopping can disrupt your budget if unplanned. By setting aside money in this category, you prevent these surprises from throwing everything else off.

In short, categorising your expenses this way brings structure, clarity, and balance to your budget. It ensures your needs are met, your future is secured, and your present is enjoyed—without letting one area take over the others.

Here's a shorter version:

- Fixed Expenses / Bills – Rent, EMIs, insurance, school fees, etc.
- Savings & Investments – Emergency funds, mutual funds, recurring deposits, etc.
- Variable Essentials / Necessities – Groceries, utilities, transport, etc.
- Lifestyle/Fun Money– Dining out, shopping, entertainment.
- Irregular/One-Time – Gifting, celebrations, travel, etc.

These categories can be customised according to your lifestyle. If you're a freelancer, maybe you need a category for professional expenses. If you have pets, include pet care. The idea is to make it reflect your real life—not someone else's ideal.

Below, I have given you a list of the most common essentials. Write down the amount beside each row. Add or delete any head if you have to. It's your budget, customise it according to your needs.

Bills	Amount (₹)
Housing & Utilities	
Rent / Home Loan EMI	
Electricity Bill	
Water Bill	
Gas (Cylinder/Piped)	
Internet & Wi-Fi	
Mobile Bills	
Apartment Maintenance	
Home Maintenance	
School / College Fees	
Tuition / Coaching Classes	
School Books & Stationery	
Uniforms & School Supplies	
Credit Card Bills	
Car / Bike EMI	
Vehicle Maintenance	
Health Insurance Premiums	

Life Insurance Premiums	
Personal Loan Repayments	
Business Loan Repayment	
Any Other Loan	
Money You Owe Anyone	
Total	

Next comes your savings. Before listing down the essentials, make a habit of paying yourself first. Below, I have listed for you the most common avenues of savings a person should invest in. Add or delete rows according to your preference, as said earlier.

Savings	**Amount (₹)**
SIP	
Mutual Funds	
Stocks	
Gold	
Recurring Deposit	
PPF	
ELSS	
National Savings Certificate (NSC)	
Post Office Savings Schemes	
EPF	
Sovereign Gold Bonds	
Bank Fixed Deposits	
Corporate Fixed Deposits	
ETFs	

Crypto	
Real Estate	
Total	

Next, list out the essentials. Here, we need to deep dive as much as possible. Overspending on essentials is the easiest budgeting mistake people make. People often have an emotional weakness towards essentials because, after all, they are "ESSENTIALS". For example, people never want to see their loved ones cut back on meals or comfort because of a poorly planned budget. Sometimes, out of love and emotion, they may even spend a little more than intended—just to see a smile or fulfil a small wish. This is ok sometimes, but this pattern tends to repeat, and it can sabotage our budget. Below, I have broken down a family's essentials into the easiest categories possible. Add or delete headings if you have to. But writing them down is of utmost importance.

Essentials	**Amount (₹)**
Fish and Meat	
Fruits & Vegetables	
Milk & Dairy Products	
Packaged Foods & Beverages	
Education & Child Expenses	
Extracurricular Activities	
Doctor Consultations	
Medicines & Pharmacy	
Gym & Fitness	

Transportation & Vehicle Expenses	
Public Transport (Metro, Bus, Auto)	
Petrol / Diesel / CNG	
Vehicle Maintenance	
Parking Fees & Tolls	
Household & Personal Care	
Domestic Help (Maid, Cook, Driver)	
Laundry & Dry Cleaning	
Home Cleaning	
New Clothing	
Pocket Money	
Pet Care	
Total	

Next, we are going to separate the fun money from our salary. Remember, this section is only applicable for fund allocation if the earlier three sections have already had their fill. Fun money is discretionary, and some months you might have to allocate very little to this section if the situation demands, or you might have to skip it altogether for the sake of financial discipline. There are times when we may need to skip the fun money section in our budget—not because it's unimportant, but because certain months bring unexpected expenses or tighter income. Maybe there's a medical bill, a home repair, or a festival around the corner that requires extra funds. The fund may be too little to disturb our emergency fund, or it may be in excess of it. In such moments, fun money takes a backseat so that essentials and priorities are covered first. It's a temporary pause, not a permanent cut, made with the understanding that joy can be postponed—but peace of mind can't.

Fun	**Amount (₹)**
Eating Out / Takeaways	
Spa & Leisure	
Movies, Concerts & Events	
Vacations & Travel	
Hobbies & Recreational Activities	
New Books	
Parlour	
Beauty & Grooming	
Long Drives	
Wishlist Items	
Total	

Next, you need to check if your budget meets the basic 50-30-20 rule. If not, you will have to work towards it. I have already talked about the 50-30-20 rule. But let us break it down further.

First and foremost, 20% of your budget should pay your Bills:

Reserved for all your fixed, recurring financial obligations—such as rent, loan EMIs, utilities, insurance premiums, school fees, and any subscriptions. These are your non-negotiables that should be paid first to avoid penalties or service disruptions.

Big bills can be bullies. They sit in the background, waiting to surprise you. Don't give them that power. Pay your rent, EMIs, school fees, and insurance premiums as soon as you receive your salary. Getting these out of the way early gives you a clear picture of what you have left. There's no worse feeling than realising mid-month that a big bill is still pending and your money is already gone. Prioritise them. Always

And then the next 30% should pay for your Essentials:

This category covers your basic day-to-day living needs like groceries, transport, fuel, basic medical expenses, household items, and other must-have expenses. While slightly flexible, this section should be monitored to avoid overspending.

This constitutes 50% of your budget. Divided into 20% for bills and 30% for essentials.

The next 25% should go into Savings:

This is your investment in the future. Whether you're saving for an emergency fund, a vacation, a home, or retirement, this portion ensures your money is growing and your goals are within reach. Consider dividing it into short-term and long-term savings or investment buckets.

Another 5% should go into One-Time Expenses:

These are the irregular yet predictable costs that sneak up on you—birthday gifts, festival shopping, yearly fees, minor repairs, or new school supplies. By contributing a little every month, you're prepared when these moments arrive.

And the last 20% should be your Fun Money:

Life isn't just about paying bills and saving—this section is for joy and relaxation. Use this for entertainment, eating out, shopping, hobbies, or weekend getaways. Having a set amount helps you enjoy life guilt-free without hurting your financial health.

Stick to this rule (as much as you can), and you will never let money control you.

I'm sure you have heard of the phrase "Cash is King"; whoever said it, it has immense importance on our financial discipline. Digital payments are great, but there's a charm—and discipline—in using cash. When you spendcash, you feel the expense more tangibly. That sense of "I'm handing over real money" creates a mental pause, helping you rethink impulse buys. It's not about avoiding digital; it's about slowing down your spending and becoming more mindful. Cash also helps when budgeting for small, everyday items. You can even divide your cash into envelopes: one for food, one for travel, one for kids' pocket money, and so on.

Using cash envelopes is a simple yet powerful way to take control of your spending. The method involves physically dividing your money into separate envelopes based on different budget categories—like groceries, transport, eating out, or fun money. Once the cash in an envelope is used up, that's it for the month. This hands-on approach creates a clear boundary that helps prevent overspending and builds real-time awareness of where your money is going. For example, if you set aside ₹3,000 for groceries and you're down to your last ₹500, you naturally start prioritising what you buy. There's no tapping a card and forgetting later. It also brings mindfulness to your budget—seeing money physically leave your hands makes every purchase more intentional. Cash envelopes are especially helpful for variable expenses that tend to go out of control. Fixed costs like rent or EMIs can be handled digitally, but envelopes work wonders for everyday spending. Over time, this method trains discipline and accountability. And while digital tools are convenient, many people find the tactile feel of using real cash more grounding and effective. It's a simple system, but when used consistently, it can completely transform the way you manage your money. This old-school method still works wonders.

Plan how much cash you'll need for things like local market shopping, public transport, tiffin, or any expense that doesn't go through an app or card. Withdrawing cash once every week or fortnight can help you track and limit your spending better. It's visual—you *see* the money leave your wallet. That makes a huge difference.

Lastly, check with your family if they have missed any bills. Money management isn't a solo job if you live with family. Talk to your partner, parents, or even your kids (if they're old enough).

Ask:

"Has any bill been missed?"

"Is there any upcoming payment I don't know about?"

"Do we need to top up anything—like school canteen fees or mobile recharges?"

This conversation can prevent a lot of confusion, last-minute borrowing, or budget blow-ups. It also creates a sense of shared responsibility, which is always a good thing.

Next, set Spending Checkpoints on Day 7, 15, and 25. Divide your essentials money by 4.3; this is a smart budgeting trick to make your monthly budget feel more manageable and realistic week by week. Here's how it works: instead of spending your entire essentials budget—like groceries, fuel, and basic household items—all at once, you divide the total by 4.3, which is the average number of weeks in a month. This gives you a weekly spending limit that helps you stay in control and avoid running out of money before the month ends.

For example, if you've allocated ₹12,900 for essentials, dividing it by 4.3 gives you approximately ₹3,000 per week. Now, you know exactly how much you can spend each week without dipping into money meant for later. This method reduces the chances of overspending early in the month and scrambling in the last few days. Budgeting isn't a one-time activity. Now, set three checkpoints in your month and allocate this money to each checkpoint. Note how the leftover money automatically adjusts to Day 31

Divide your spending accordingly:

- ₹3000 from Day 1 to 7
- ₹3000 from Day 8 to 15

- ₹3000 from Day 16 to 25
- ₹3000 from Day 26–30
- ₹ 900 for Day 31

This rhythm creates structure and control—your two best friends in the world of money.

- Day 7: Check if you're on track. Too much spent too early? Slow down.
- Day 15: Halfway review. Adjust if needed.
- Day 25: Wrap-up plan. Make sure essentials are covered till the next payday.

At each checkpoint, compare what you've spent with what you planned. If you're under budget—great! If you've gone over—adjust in the next segment. These mini-reviews help you course-correct without guilt or panic. You start planning your grocery runs, fuel refills, and other purchases with more awareness. And if you underspend one week, you can carry the extra forward. It's a small shift in mindset, but it turns your monthly money into bite-sized, manageable portions, making budgeting feel less overwhelming and more effective.

Designing your budget is like designing your month. It may seem like a small task, but it has a powerful ripple effect on your entire financial life. The time you spend during Days 2 and 3 is an investment—a quiet, thoughtful session where you take back control. Remember, your budget is not a punishment. It's not a cage. It's a plan, a guide, a tool to help you spend wisely, save steadily, and live peacefully.

So, sit down, grab your favourite pen or budgeting app, and let's start giving every rupee a mission. You've got this!

☑ Key Takeaways From This Chapter

- Budgeting gives every rupee a mission, a home, a purpose, and a plan.
- Bad budgets create financial chaos through overspending and missed expenses.
- List all income sources clearly to build a strong foundation.
- Categorise expenses into Bills, Savings, Essentials, Fun, and One-Time for clarity.
- Prioritise Bills and Savings first before lifestyle spending.
- Follow the 50-30-20 framework with small tweaks for your situation.
- Use cash or envelopes for essentials and variable spending to stay disciplined.
- Set checkpoints (Day 7, 15, 25) to track and adjust spending mid-month.
- Involve your family to avoid missed payments and build shared responsibility.
- Budgeting is not a restriction—it's a tool for freedom, peace, and mindful living.

Exercises for You

1. Take 5 envelopes, label them Bills, Savings, Essentials, Fun, and One-Time. Put cash into each based on your budget. Physically handling money makes spending limits more real.

2. Write down your monthly income on sticky notes. Place them on a table. Now "spend" each note by moving it into piles for expenses. Seeing the piles shrink gives a clear visual of money flow.
3. Divide essential money into 4 jars (Week 1, Week 2, Week 3, Week 4). Each week, use only that jar. This tactile method helps practice restraint.
4. Gather your family and go through the expense sheet together. Let each member add their inputs (school fees, groceries, subscriptions). It builds responsibility and prevents missed bills.
5. Withdraw your weekly essentials money in cash. Every time you pay, note it down on a mini notepad. Review at the end of the week—did you overspend or save?

CHAPTER 4

GROCERY PLANNING LIKE A FRENCH CHEF (DAY 4)

Intentional Grocery Spending That Saves Thousands

Purpose of the Chapter:

To turn everyday grocery shopping into a mindful, budget-conscious ritual. This chapter teaches readers how to treat groceries with the same discipline and finesse as a French chef—planning, preparing, and purchasing with intent, not impulse.

What You'll Learn in This Chapter:

- How to budget for groceries without sacrificing quality
- The value of menu planning and pantry auditing
- Understanding the psychology of supermarket layouts
- Techniques for reducing food waste and repetitive purchases
- Creating a grocery shopping system that's sustainable and satisfying

"Grocery planning is not just about food—it's about self-control and financial artistry."

CHAPTER IV

GROCERY PLANNING LIKE A FRENCH CHEF (DAY 4)

> *The health of your family is a journey that begins at the grocery store. Plan the journey carefully.*

There's something incredibly charming about the way French chefs approach food. They don't just cook; they plan, curate, and select each ingredient with intention and artistry. Imagine if you applied a little bit of that magic to your own grocery planning. Instead of chaotic, last-minute dashes to the supermarket, you'd be moving with the grace and calm of someone who knows exactly what they need, when they need it, and how much they'll use. Welcome to Day 4 of your financial journey — Grocery Planning Like a French Chef.

Budget meal planning isn't about eating boring meals or cutting back to the point of deprivation. It's about maximising flavours, health, and joy while keeping your wallet happy. A good plan ensures that every rupee you spend on food serves a purpose — whether nourishing your family, saving you time or even giving you the simple pleasure of a well-cooked meal at the end of a long day. Today, we'll learn how to grocery plan like pros — where everything has its place, nothing is wasted, and even a simple dal-chawal feels gourmet.

Let's be brutally honest for a moment — most of us are leaking money through poor grocery habits without even realising it. Imagine this: It's 7 PM, you're tired from work, and you realise you're out of vegetables. You open your favourite grocery app and order a few things hastily. Delivery charges, premium prices for convenience, and minimum order values that force you to buy things you didn't need — all quietly inflate your bill.

Think about Shalu, a 30-year-old working professional. She thought she was being smart by doing "quick" online grocery orders twice a week. At the end of the month, she noticed ₹3000 more on her grocery bill compared to her friend, who shopped once a week at the local market. The culprit? Delivery fees, impulse buys encouraged by "you might also like" recommendations, and ordering small quantities often.

Improper planning leads to last-minute, expensive solutions. Ordering when hungry or tired leads to costly mistakes. We don't just lose money; we lose peace of mind, too. Learning to plan properly brings back control — and savings. Believe it or not, just a little bit of planning can slice 20–30% off your grocery bill without you even feeling the pinch. Here's how it works: when you plan meals, you buy exactly what you need. You use perishables before they go bad. You make fewer trips to the store, cutting down on impulse buys.

***Pro-tip**: Always plan grocery shopping when you are relaxed, not tired or hungry. A calm mind makes better buying decisions.*

Let's take another example — Sameer's family of four spent ₹10,000 on groceries each month. After implementing structured planning — weekly shopping lists, meal prepping on Sundays, and using frozen leftovers — his grocery bill dropped to ₹7,500 without any sacrifice in the quality of meals. Over a year, that's ₹30,000 saved — enough for a short vacation or a hefty contribution to a savings goal.

Small changes stack up quickly. Buying seasonal veggies, avoiding processed foods, and cooking in batches are simple strategies that add up to significant savings.

Grocery planning isn't just about your wallet. It directly impacts your health and the planet. When you plan meals intentionally, you include more vegetables, whole grains, and home-cooked dishes instead of last-minute unhealthy takeout. You also waste less food. Without planning, you end up with a fridge full of slimy spinach, forgotten yoghurt, and half-used sauces that eventually hit the trash. With proper planning, everything gets used. Your meals are fresher, and your carbon footprint shrinks.

Think about it this way: if a French chef walked into your kitchen, would they find a beautiful array of fresh produce ready to be transformed? Or a sad graveyard of expired dairy and wilting greens? The choice is yours.

One of the first steps to better grocery planning is to treat your pantry like a mini grocery store. Imagine neat shelves, clear categories, and visible labels. When you can see what you already have, you don't buy unnecessary duplicates. When your pantry is a mess, you shop based on doubt. "Do I have cumin? Maybe not, better get some just in case." Multiply that uncertainty across all your items, and you're throwing away thousands a year on things you already have.

> ***Pro-tip:*** *Dedicate 10 minutes every Sunday to pantry checks. This habit prevents overbuying.*

Organising doesn't need to be fancy. Just group similar items together — grains, spices, canned goods, snacks — and keep track of what's low. It's the foundation of strategic shopping and meal planning.

Labelling isn't just for perfectionists. It's practical, and it saves money. When you bring groceries home, quickly label items with notes like "Eat First," "Use in 3 Days," or "Use Within a Week." Or instead of labelling, keep them in different places/shelves so you know what will go bad first, so to can eat them first. This visual cue helps you prioritise what needs to be eaten and when. Instead of discovering a sad, mouldy bunch of coriander a week later, you'll use it up in a chutney within a day or two. Even a simple whiteboard in your kitchen listing "Urgent Use Items" works wonders. In the busy flow of life, small visual reminders prevent food wastage.

Your grocery plan should reflect your family's actual consumption, not some idealised Pinterest version of meal prepping. A family of six eats differently from a couple.

A good thumb rule is: per person, about 2.5kg of fruits and vegetables per week. Factor in children's snacks, adult meals, and special dietary needs like high-protein diets.

If your family loves snacking, allocate more for quick foods like carrots, cucumbers, and bananas. If you have teenagers, double the protein and carb portions! Planning according to real consumption patterns prevents both shortages and overbuying.

Here's a simple rule to streamline your grocery budget: 60% should go toward essentials like grains, vegetables, milk, and pulses; 30% toward semi-essential items like snacks, ready-to-cook foods, and luxury items; and 10% for treats like ice creams, chocolates, or imported foods. It keeps your basics covered, allows for enjoyment, and still prioritises smart spending. Like a French chef who spends most of their budget on quality produce and proteins — and only a little on indulgences.

Festivals bring joy, but they also bring chaos to your grocery budget if you're not careful. During these times, groceries — especially dry fruits, sweets, and gifts — become premium priced. Plan the festival needs in advance. Buy dry fruits and ghee a month early when prices are stable. Budget a festive fund each month if possible. Also, expect that meal routines will be disrupted — plan lighter home meals between feasts to balance health and budget.

Think like a chef who pre-orders rare ingredients before the holiday rushes.

Buying in bulk can be a blessing if done smartly. Items like rice, wheat, sugar, dal, and cooking oil are much cheaper when bought in larger quantities. Plus, it saves you time and reduces packaging waste. But beware of the "10-for-1" trap — flashy deals on perishable goods where you get tempted to buy ten when you only need two. Bulk only works if the shelf life matches your consumption rate.

> ***Pro-tip:*** *Match bulk purchases with consumption speed. If in doubt, buy smaller packs.*

Buying 10 kilograms of onions is smart if your family eats onions daily. But ten tubs of yoghurt? Disaster!

If you live in a close-knit neighbourhood, consider forming a buying co-op. Pool together to buy bulk items like grains, oil, and cleaning supplies. Split the quantities and the savings. It builds community ties and leverages buying power. For instance, buying 50kg of rice directly from a mill might cost ₹30/kg instead of ₹45/kg at retail prices. Sharing it among five families brings the cost and quantity to manageable levels for everyone.

It's how smart communities have saved for centuries — and you can too.

One of the easiest and most delicious ways to save money on groceries is to eat seasonally. Seasonal produce is fresher, more flavorful, and significantly cheaper because it's available in abundance. It hasn't been stored, transported long distances, or artificially ripened, which means you're getting better quality at a lower price.

Think of summer when markets overflow with mangoes and cucumbers. Or winter, when carrots, spinach, and cauliflower are everywhere. Compare the cost of tomatoes in peak season versus during off-season monsoons — it can double. French chefs always work with seasonal ingredients because they understand nature's rhythm and want the best flavours.

Here's a small case: Anita, a home cook in Pune, started switching her weekly menu based on what the local market offered at the lowest prices. Over six months, she saved ₹400–₹600 monthly. More importantly, her food became more diverse, colourful, and nutritionally rich. Seasonal food is not just good economics; it's smart cooking.

I have listed all the seasonal fruits and vegetables below. Take inspiration from the chart.

Season	Vegetables	Region Notes
Spring	Bottle Gourd (Lauki)	**All India**, especially North & Central
(Mar-May)	Ridge Gourd (Turai)	
	Cucumber (Kheera)	
	Pumpkin (Kaddu)	
	Green Beans (Fansi)	
	Cluster Beans (Gawar)	
	Raw Mango (Kaccha Aam)	
	Spinach (Palak – early)	

Summer	Okra (Bhindi)	**West & South**: Better for gourds
(Jun–Aug)	Brinjal (Baingan)	**East**: Parwal, Petha
	Tomato (Tamatar)	
	Snake Gourd (Chichinda)	
	Ash Gourd (Petha)	
	Pointed Gourd (Parwal)	
	Amaranth Greens (Chaulai)	
	Kantola (Spiny Gourd)	
Monsoon	Colocasia Leaves (Arbi Patta)	**East**: Poi Saag, Arbi Patta
(Jul–Sep)	Indian Spinach (Poi Saag)	**North**: Corn & Yam
	Corn (Bhutta)	
	Yam (Suran)	
	Taro Root (Arbi)	
	Pumpkin (Kaddu)	
Autumn	Carrot (Gajar)	**North & West**: Root veggies dominate
(Oct–Nov)	Radish (Mooli)	
	Turnip (Shalgam)	
	Sweet Potato (Shakarkand)	
	Fenugreek (Methi)	
	Coriander (Dhaniya)	
	Beetroot (Chukandar)	

Winter	Cauliflower (Phool Gobi)	
(Dec–Feb)	Cabbage (Patta Gobi)	
	Peas (Matar)	
	Desi Carrot (Gajar)	
	Radish (Mooli)	
	Spinach (Palak)	
	Mustard Greens (Sarson)	
	Bathua	
	Green Garlic (Hara Lehsun)	

Season	Fruits	Region Notes
Spring (Mar-May)	Papaya, Banana, Pineapple, Watermelon, Musk Melon, Wood Apple (Bael)	**South & Central India** – Watermelon, Pineapple
		North India – Bael
Summer (Jun-Aug)	Mango, Jamun, Litchi, Jackfruit, Guava, Banana, Ice Apple (Tadgola)	**North** – Mango, Litchi, Jamun
		South – Jackfruit, Ice Apple
		East – Guava
Monsoon (Jul-Sep)	Pear, Plums, Jamun, Guava, Banana, Papaya	**North & East** – Pears, Plums
		South – Banana, Papaya

<table>
<tr><td rowspan="2">Autumn (Oct-Nov)</td><td rowspan="2">Pomegranate, Custard Apple (Sitaphal), Guava, Apple (early), Banana</td><td>West – Custard Apple</td></tr>
<tr><td>North – Pomegranate, Guava</td></tr>
<tr><td rowspan="3">Winter (Dec-Feb)</td><td rowspan="3">Orange, Apple, Amla, Carambola (Star Fruit), Chikoo, Guava, Dates (fresh)</td><td>North – Apple, Orange, Amla</td></tr>
<tr><td>West – Chikoo</td></tr>
<tr><td>South – Star Fruit</td></tr>
</table>

While grocery apps offer convenience, they almost always come at a premium. When you start calculating delivery charges, price markups, and minimum order fillers, the total cost shoots up. A better solution? Fix a reliable local vendor or sabziwala who can deliver regularly.

In many Indian households, a dedicated errand boy, local vegetable vendor, or fish/meat seller is a time-tested solution. They offer better prices, fresher goods, and flexibility. You can ask for ripeness levels, mix and match quantities, or even pay weekly. The relationship builds trust and often leads to discounts or freebies. Instead of one-size-fits-all delivery apps, use specialised vendors: one for vegetables, one for meat, and one for fish. Each has better rates than apps that consolidate and charge commissions. Plus, local suppliers are more likely to understand your family's taste preferences and suggest the freshest options.

Versatility is the holy grail of budget cooking. Ingredients that work in multiple dishes reduce waste and make planning easy. A "5 in 1" ingredient is one you can use in five different ways.

Take onions: they go in curries, pulao, omelettes, chutneys, and sandwiches. Tomatoes? Same story. Paneer can become bhurji, curry, sandwiches, parathas, or a salad topping. Potatoes? Unlimited options. These ingredients offer value through flexibility. When planning your grocery list, think of how many ways you can use each item. Buying items that serve multiple purposes ensures everything gets used. It also helps when you're running low — you can whip up a meal without needing something specific.

Chefs always keep a few base ingredients that work across cuisines — that's the secret to their low-waste, high-efficiency kitchens.

One trick French chefs often use is batch cooking — and freezing. Making a double batch of rajma or chhole takes just a few extra minutes but gives you meals for later in the week. Freezable dishes save time, reduce daily cooking fatigue, and help you avoid unnecessary takeout. Good freezer-friendly dishes include soups, dals, stews, koftas, kababs, cutlets, and even fully prepped parathas. Store them in labelled containers with the date so you can rotate them efficiently.

> ***Pro-tip:*** *Freeze in single-meal portions. It prevents wastage and makes reheating quicker.*

Let's say you cook on Sunday and freeze three dishes. On a busy Thursday, instead of ordering pizza, you just reheat a home-cooked meal in minutes. That's money saved and health preserved.

Pro-tip: *Snack Before You Shop and Use a Small Basket*

Ever noticed how you suddenly crave chips, chocolates, and cookies while shopping on an empty stomach? Shopping when hungry leads to emotional and impulsive purchases. A snack beforehand — a banana, a cup of tea, a biscuit — helps you stay focused.

Another subtle trick is using a smaller basket instead of a trolley. Limited space makes you prioritise essentials. Studies show shoppers buy 30–40% more with large trolleys than with baskets, purely because of space psychology. When you are alert, fed, and holding a small basket, you're more likely to buy what you actually need — not what marketing wants you to.

Sales aren't just for clothes or electronics. Groceries, especially packaged items, go on sale often. But the key is planning around the discounts — not falling for them impulsively. Make it a habit to check store flyers, WhatsApp vendor messages, or your local supermarket's weekly deals. If you see a good price on something you use regularly — tea, rice, biscuits — stock up within reason.

However, avoid the trap of buying discounted items you don't normally use. If you don't eat cornflakes, don't buy a giant box just because it's 50% off. Smart shopping is about saving on your regular items, not hoarding unnecessary ones.

A good weekly meal plan balances heavy and light meals. It gives your body rest, your stomach variety, and your kitchen breathing room.

For example, after a heavy biryani dinner, plan a light khichdi and sabzi meal the next day. Follow up paneer butter masala night with a simple vegetable stir-fry. Not every meal has to be a feast.

Theme days help too: Meatless Mondays, Tiffin Tuesdays, One-pot Wednesdays, South Indian Thursdays, etc. This adds structure and fun to your planning. French chefs build variety across a week — not every meal is rich. Mimic that balance in your home cooking.

Gas and electricity are hidden grocery costs. The longer your cooking time, the more your bill. Pressure cookers are your best friends. They reduce cooking time drastically and preserve nutrients. One whistle for rice, two for dal, three for potatoes — that's faster, cheaper, and cleaner than long-boiling stovetop methods. You can also use it for meat stews, pulao, and even upma.

Minimal ingredient recipes like thepla, dhokla, aloo sabzi, poha, and chilla are perfect for mid-week meals. They're filling, quick, and low on energy use. These are the real budget meals — low cost, high nutrition, and loved by all.

Prices are never constant. A smart shopper adapts. If tomatoes shoot up to ₹100/kg, switch to tamarind or curd-based curries for a while. When spinach is cheap, make palak-based dishes more often. Track prices once a week. If something becomes too expensive, drop it temporarily from your meal plan. Replace imported ingredients with local substitutes. This flexibility is what makes you a grocery genius.

Just like chefs adjust menus based on market availability, you should adjust your plans based on price trends. It keeps the budget intact without sacrificing quality.

Start by writing down your average monthly grocery spend for the last three months. Now, as you implement better planning, note down each grocery expense — either in a diary or on a simple Excel sheet.

Add categories like vegetables, dry groceries, meat, snacks, etc. At the end of each month, compare with your past data. You'll start seeing where you saved — and where you still overspent.

Even a ₹500 monthly saving is ₹6,000 a year. Track it. Celebrate it. Use it for something meaningful.

Grocery Checklist

A solid checklist saves time and money. Break it into categories:

- **Vegetables**: potatoes, onions, tomatoes, carrots, spinach
- **Fruits**: bananas, apples, oranges
- **Grains & Pulses**: rice, atta, chana dal, moong dal
- **Dairy**: milk, curd, paneer, butter
- **Spices & Condiments**: turmeric, chilli powder, mustard seeds
- **Frozen or Ready Items**: parathas, green peas
- **Non-veg (if applicable)**: chicken, fish, eggs
- **Snacks & Extras**: biscuits, tea, coffee, cup noodles.

Think in categories + quantities.

Vegetables (Weekly): potatoes (2kg), onions (2kg), tomatoes (1kg), carrots (500g), spinach (2 bunches)
Fruits (Weekly): bananas (12 pcs), apples (1kg), oranges (1kg)
Grains & Pulses (Monthly): rice (5kg), atta (10kg), chana dal (2kg), moong dal (2kg)
Dairy (Weekly): milk (5L), curd (2kg), paneer (500g), butter (200g)
Spices & Condiments: turmeric (100g), chilli powder (100g), mustard seeds (100g)
Frozen/Ready: peas (500g), parathas (1 pack)
Protein: chicken (2kg), fish (1kg), eggs (1 tray)
Snacks & Extras: biscuits (2 packs), tea (500g), coffee (200g), cup noodles (2 packs)
Customise your list based on your habits. Print it. Laminate it. Stick it to your fridge.

Sample Meal Plan Using the Above Knowledge

Monday:

Lunch – Moong dal + rice + cucumber salad

Dinner – Dhokla + mint chutney + buttermilk

Tuesday:

Lunch – Aloo gobi + roti + curd

Dinner – Palak paneer + jeera rice

Wednesday:

Lunch – Vegetable pulao + papad

Dinner – Upma + sambhar + carrot sticks

Thursday:

Lunch – Chana masala + rice

Dinner – Chilla + coconut chutney + boiled eggs

Friday:

Lunch – Masoor dal + beetroot sabzi + paratha

Dinner – Homemade chicken curry + roti

Saturday:

Lunch – Khichdi + pickle + raita

Dinner – Pulao from frozen veggies + fried fish

Sunday:

Lunch – Light salad + soup

Dinner – Eating out (treat within budget!)

> ***Pro-tip****: Always cook 1 extra portion at dinner. Leftovers make the next day's lunch easier and cheaper.*

After all that being said, please remember that even the most well-planned kitchen needs a break. Eating out once a week helps avoid monotony and gives the cook some rest. Choose affordable options — a local South Indian joint, a thali place, or a good-value café. Set a monthly eating-out budget. Instead of random indulgences, treat it like a reward. Sunday outings also become family rituals — something everyone looks forward to.

A French chef takes pride in cooking, but even they enjoy a fine meal made by someone else now and then.

Grocery planning, when done right, is more than a budgeting tool — it's a lifestyle upgrade. It transforms your kitchen from a chaotic place of waste into an organised, joyful space where every ingredient matters and every rupee is respected.

Planning like a French chef isn't about fancy sauces or imported cheese. It's about respect — for food, money, and the people you cook for. With your pantry in order, your meals planned, your suppliers in place, and your money flowing with purpose, you're no longer just surviving the month. You're thriving through it.

Day 4 is a turning point — from here, every bite you eat and every rupee you spend is a conscious, empowering choice.

Bon appétit and budget well!

☑ Key Takeaways From This Chapter

- Grocery planning saves **20–30% of food costs** and reduces waste.
- **Impulse buys and delivery charges** inflate bills when shopping without a plan.
- A **well-organised pantry** prevents duplicate purchases and food spoilage.

- **Meal planning based on real family consumption** avoids shortages and excess.
- Follow the **60–30–10 budgeting rule** for essentials, semi-essentials, and treats.
- **Bulk buying works only for long-lasting staples**, not perishables.
- **Seasonal produce** is fresher, cheaper, and more nutritious.
- Building ties with **local vendors** ensures better prices and quality.
- **Versatile ingredients** like onions, tomatoes, and paneer cut waste.
- **Batch cooking and freezing** saves time, money, and energy.
- Smart habits like **snacking before shopping and using baskets** reduce overspending.
- **Sales are helpful only for regular items**, not unnecessary ones.
- A **weekly meal plan** balances nutrition, cost, and cooking effort.
- **Pressure cookers and quick recipes** lower fuel and electricity costs.
- Stay **flexible with substitutes** when prices spike.
- **Tracking expenses monthly** highlights savings and overspending patterns.
- A **checklist and sample meal plan** make shopping structured and stress-free.

- Occasional **budgeted eating-out** prevents monotony and offers balance.
- Grocery planning is not just financial—it's a **lifestyle upgrade** rooted in respect for food, money, and family.

✍ Exercises for You

1. Take everything out of your pantry, group by category, and label. This physical act reinforces organization habits.
2. Next time at the market, note the prices of 5 seasonal vegetables. Write them in a notebook and compare weekly.
3. Do one week of grocery shopping using only a hand basket, not a trolley. Reflect on how much less you spent.
4. Cook one extra dish this week, freeze it, and reheat it after 3 days. Note the time and money saved.
5. Involve kids or family by giving them ₹500 imaginary rupees to plan a mini grocery list. Compare it with real costs.

CHAPTER 5

FINANCIAL HOUSEKEEPING (DAYS 5 TO 7)

Decluttering Your Financial Life for Peace and Power

Purpose of the Chapter:

To introduce the concept of "financial housekeeping," helping readers identify, clean up, and streamline all aspects of their money-related life, from physical clutter to emotional baggage. It's about resetting systems, tools, and mental patterns.

What You'll Learn in This Chapter:

- How to declutter financial paperwork, apps, and subscriptions
- Reviewing and simplifying bank accounts and digital wallets
- Understanding financial leaks, lazy decisions, and toxic money habits
- Organising financial priorities like a minimalist
- How less financial mess = more mental clarity

"You don't need more income—you need less chaos."

CHAPTER V

FINANCIAL HOUSEKEEPING (DAYS 5 TO 7)

"

Financial decluttering is not about giving up what you love—it's about removing what no longer serves you, so your money flows toward the life you truly want.

When most of us hear "housekeeping," our minds immediately go to mops, dusters, and a nagging weekend chore list. But financial housekeeping? That often sounds vague or—worse—unnecessary. Yet, this quiet, overlooked aspect of personal finance may be the difference between living paycheck-to-paycheck and feeling confident, calm, and in control.

Think of financial housekeeping as a spring-cleaning session for your money. It involves reviewing your financial habits, sorting and organising bills and documents, eliminating clutter (both digital and physical), and tightening up areas where you're leaking money without realising it. It's not just about cutting costs or saving more—it's about clarity. It's about making your financial environment as clean, organised, and calm as your ideal living room.

The importance of financial housekeeping cannot be overstated. You could have the most detailed budget, a solid income, and all the right intentions—but if your financial records are scattered, if auto-debits you've forgotten about are draining your account, or if you've got duplicate services billing you silently in the background, your financial ship could slowly start to sink without you noticing.

And that's exactly why Days 5 to 7 are dedicated to this: decluttering, checking, organising, and realigning. It's the kind of work that doesn't always feel urgent but pays you back in peace of mind and financial stability.

The key here is consistency and attention. These days are your reset button—your way of making sure your plans from Days 1 to 4 are being supported, not sabotaged, by overlooked details.

In the sections that follow, you'll walk through practical steps to assess and improve your financial hygiene. Whether you live alone, with roommates, or as part of a large family, this chapter will help you reimagine what "housekeeping" truly means—far beyond dustpans and into the heart of smart, intentional living.

We're just five days into the month, but it's already time for a quick check-in. This isn't a full budget analysis—that will come later. Instead, this is like stepping on the financial weighing scale just to see how you're trending.

By now, if you've followed the steps from Days 1 to 4, you would have already created your budget and allocated funds across categories like groceries, rent, utilities, transportation, debt repayments, savings, and a little fun. Now, pause and take ten minutes to compare your actual spending against your planned budget. Did you already overspend on groceries? Were there some impulse purchases? Maybe your UPI transactions show a bit of emotional spending that crept in after a long day. It happens—and this review isn't about blame. It's about catching deviations early.

Let's take the example of Priya, a 29-year-old freelance designer from Pune. She budgeted ₹4,000 for groceries but ended up spending ₹6,200 in the first five days thanks to a sale on imported snacks she "just had to try." When she did her Day 5 review, she was shocked but thankful—had she not caught it early, she would have continued spending freely. She adjusted her discretionary spending and meal prepped the rest of the month to rebalance.

This small review is your chance to correct the course before the rest of the month gallops away. Look at your bank statement, digital wallet history, and receipts. Is your budget tracking well, or are some categories bleeding? This one exercise, repeated monthly, can save you from the "how did I run out of money?" panic that hits around Day 20. Repeat this step on days 15, 20 and 25.

Remember, your budget is a living document. It can be tweaked and improved with insights from your real-world behaviour. And that's the real power of this mini-review—it grounds your plan in reality.

> ***Pro-tip**: Treat your budget like a Google Map—it reroutes when you take a wrong turn, but only if you keep it updated.*

One of the simplest yet most powerful ways to take charge of your spending is to create limits, not just in your mind but through actual tools and tech. Technology has given us an enormous advantage when it comes to financial discipline, yet we often leave it underutilised.

Start with your UPI apps—Google Pay, PhonePe, Paytm, whichever one you use the most. These apps allow you to set daily or monthly spending limits. Most people aren't even aware of this feature. Use it. If you tend to order food when stressed, and your UPI record shows four Swiggy or Zomato hits in a week, set a weekly cap for food delivery. When you reach that cap, the app will stop you from further transactions—your digital wallet becomes your accountability buddy.

Next, check your bank account's online dashboard. Many banks allow you to set daily transfer limits or freeze certain types of transfers temporarily. It sounds like overkill, but if you're someone who finds money "disappearing," these tools act as speed bumps, giving you a moment to reflect before hitting send.

Credit cards are trickier. You can't usually adjust your credit limit easily unless you request a change from the bank. But what you can do is set your own internal cap. Say your limit is ₹1,00,000—but you know you can't handle more than ₹15,000 in monthly charges. Write that number on a post-it and stick it inside your wallet or set up alerts through your credit card app to warn you when you cross ₹10,000. Treat that self-imposed limit as sacred.

Lastly, if you use cash—even occasionally—get into the habit of recording every transaction. Yes, every single chai, auto ride, and ₹50 gift. Use a small notebook or a note-taking app. This isn't about being obsessive—it's about visibility. Cash disappears faster than we think, and tracking it gives you clarity and control.

This system is what helped Arvind, a 35-year-old teacher from Indore, realise he was spending ₹3,000 a month on small, unnecessary cash purchases—mostly on snacks, soft drinks, and "just one more" Uber ride. Once he had visibility, he reduced his cash allowance and redirected the saved money into his emergency fund.

Financial discipline starts with limits. Set them. Respect them. And watch how this one practice changes everything.

> ***Pro-tip:*** *Link your limits to goals. For example, money saved by eating out less goes directly into your vacation fund.*

Auto-debit instructions are incredibly convenient—but they can also be silent saboteurs if you don't keep track. Many of us set them up once—maybe for a SIP, EMI, subscription, or utility—and then forget all about them. Over time, they quietly drain money from your account, sometimes for things you no longer use, or at amounts that have increased without you noticing.

Begin your auto-debit audit by checking your bank's net banking dashboard or mobile app. There's usually a tab that lists all standing instructions or scheduled payments. Make a note of each one: What is it for? How much is deducted? When is it scheduled?

You'll likely find a few surprises. Maybe your old gym still deducts ₹1,200 monthly. Maybe you had set up an EMI on your credit card that's been paid off, but the deduction cycle is still active. Or perhaps an old SIP in a low-performing mutual fund is running quietly in the background.

When 32-year-old Sneha from Kochi checked her auto-debits, she found a ₹99/month deduction from a mobile protection plan she'd never actually used, for a phone she no longer even owned. Over the previous year, she'd lost ₹1,188 just like that. She cancelled it that day and created a spreadsheet to track future auto-debits.

Make it a practice to review auto-debits once a month—ideally during this Day 5–7 window. And don't just cancel blindly. Some deductions—like for your emergency fund, health insurance, or utility payments—are useful. But the key is *knowing* what's being deducted, *why*, and whether it still aligns with your current life and priorities.

Most people don't know how many subscriptions they're paying for. That's the power—and the danger—of the subscription economy. Everything from movies to music, fitness apps to meditation, even PDF converters and grammar checkers now run on monthly billing models. It's death by a thousand ₹199 cuts.

Take 20 minutes today to audit your subscriptions. Go through your bank statement, your email inbox (search "subscription" or "auto-renewal"), and your phone apps. You'll be shocked at what you find.

> ***Pro-tip***: *Instead of cancelling forever, try the pause or rotate method—unsubscribe for 1–2 months, then rejoin if you truly miss it.*

Start with streaming. Are you using Netflix, Amazon Prime, Disney+ Hotstar, and SonyLIV actively? Be honest. If you're only watching one or two shows on each, can you take a break and rotate them monthly? Cancelling and resubscribing later is easier than ever.

Now check for software and apps. Tools like Grammarly, Canva Pro, Adobe, Notion, Microsoft Office, or even meditation apps like Headspace often renew silently. Are you using them? Many have free alternatives or cheaper plans. One user, Ravi, was shocked to see ₹14,000 leave his account annually for five apps he hadn't opened in six months. He cancelled three of them immediately and set a calendar reminder to review renewals every 90 days.

Also, check if you're being double-billed. Sometimes, families forget that they have multiple people paying for the same subscription—one via card, another via UPI.

You might feel reluctant to cancel a service because "what if I need it later?" But remember: subscriptions are not your identity.

You can always restart them. This small act of decluttering gives you a sense of control and saves money with almost no sacrifice.

Financial clutter is like dust—it gathers quietly in corners you stop paying attention to. Dormant accounts, unused credit cards, forgotten e-wallets, and random "just-in-case" credit lines not only take up mental space but can also be potential security risks.

Let's start with bank accounts. If you've worked in multiple cities or changed jobs over the years, chances are you've got old salary accounts still sitting idle. These may not seem like a big deal, but many banks charge maintenance fees if a minimum balance isn't maintained. Plus, they create confusion during tax filing season. Go to the bank (or use online facilities) and initiate a formal closure. Consolidate to two or three active accounts: one for spending, one for saving, and one for investments or business, if needed.

Credit cards next. Some people hold five or six cards and only actively use one or two. Each unused card is an open gateway to identity theft or fraud, especially if you don't track it. Moreover, unused cards with zero activity can affect your credit score negatively. Close the ones you don't need—but do so carefully. Make sure any dues are cleared, reward points redeemed, and that you get a formal closure certificate.

E-wallets are often overlooked. You may have balances sitting in Ola Money, Freecharge, Mobikwik, or Paytm. Log in, transfer the money to your bank account, or use it consciously.

Clean out the ones you don't use. Each active account is another set of credentials you need to protect.

Lastly, reduce unnecessary credit lines. If you've taken pre-approved loans or credit lines that you never use, talk to the bank and cancel them. They may offer a financial cushion, but they also show up on your credit report as open liabilities.

This is the part where financial courage comes into play. Most people never question the EMI they're paying, the interest rate they've agreed to, or the insurance premium they've been auto-renewing for years. But here's the thing: banks and companies *expect* most customers to be passive. That's where they make their margins. When you stop being passive, you reclaim your power.

Take loans first. If you've been paying an EMI for over a year or two, and interest rates have dropped, you might be eligible for a lower rate. You don't need to switch banks immediately. Just go to your bank and ask for a **rate revision based on current market rates**. They often have internal retention teams who can offer you a better deal rather than risk losing you to another bank. For example, a ₹25 lakh home loan reduced by even 0.5% can save you around ₹1,200 per month—that's ₹14,400 annually.

If your bank doesn't cooperate, consider **loan refinancing**. Approach another bank with a better rate, and check if they will cover the processing fee. Yes, there's paperwork involved, but the savings are real and long-term.

Now, about insurance. Whether it's term insurance, vehicle insurance, or health coverage, **don't just auto-renew blindly**. Every year, compare policies on aggregator sites like

Policybazaar or Coverfox. Many people are shocked to find that they're overpaying by ₹2,000–₹5,000 for the same coverage they could get elsewhere. Also, if you've improved your health or quit smoking, some insurers offer **revised premiums**.

Even if your vehicle insurance is bundled with your dealership, you are not obligated to renew with them. A woman in Ahmedabad saved ₹3,200 on her car's annual insurance just by switching from the dealership's default provider to an online plan with the same coverage.

This month, set aside a day to call your bank, your insurance agent, and your mobile service provider. Ask for better deals. Be polite but firm. The worst they can say is no, but very often, they say yes. And that "yes" could save you thousands over the year.

Think of this process as detoxing your digital financial life. Like a good declutter session in your home, you'll feel lighter, freer, and far more in control.

A lot of financial stress doesn't come from a lack of money—it comes from disorganisation. It's that sinking feeling when a warranty expires the day before your refrigerator stops working, or you can't find a receipt when trying to claim reimbursement or a tax deduction. These little moments pile up and become anxiety. That's where a well-maintained bill and receipt system becomes your superhero in disguise.

Now, there's no one-size-fits-all approach here. Some people love paper. Others are digital-first. The key is to pick a system that fits your lifestyle—and then actually use it.

Let's start with physical filing. Get yourself a three-folder filing system: one for household expenses, one for personal spending, and one for business-related costs (especially important if you're self-employed or freelancing). Label them clearly. Within each, use transparent sleeves or envelopes to further divide bills—electricity, water, rent, groceries, subscriptions, etc. Once a week or fortnight, take 10 minutes to file whatever receipts or bills you've accumulated. Don't toss them into a drawer. That drawer becomes a black hole.

If you're going digital—and many of us should, to save space—create folders on Google Drive, Dropbox, or your preferred cloud service. Label them exactly like the physical ones: Household, Personal, Business. Under each, create monthly folders. Take a photo or scan each bill, receipt, or invoice and upload it immediately. Name files with the date and vendor—for example: "2025-05-05_Electricity_Bill_BESCOM.jpg." This simple naming system makes future searches a breeze.

This method saved Nandini, a 40-year-old baker from Chennai, over ₹8,000 in one year. She used to toss receipts into a kitchen drawer. But after missing a few warranty claims and tax deductions, she implemented this digital filing system. Now she has peace of mind—and a perfectly organised expense trail.

The real secret? Make filing part of your weekly housekeeping routine. Do it with your Sunday coffee or as part of your Monday morning start. This tiny habit prevents enormous chaos later.

One of the most neglected areas in financial housekeeping is the maintenance and backup of essential financial documents.

We live in a time when everything from identity to property is digitised, and yet many households have papers lying in drawers without any order or backup. That's not just disorganised—it's dangerous.

Imagine this: A family in Pune faced a tough situation when the breadwinner was hospitalised suddenly. They needed the health insurance policy number to begin the claim process. But the original document was buried somewhere in a cupboard, and the soft copy was never saved. It delayed the claim by 10 days. In emergencies, every hour counts.

This is why every Indian household must have a verified and backed-up set of financial documents. Let's go through the most important ones:

1. **Aadhaar Card and PAN Card** – These are needed for nearly every financial transaction in India. Keep both soft and hard copies.
2. **Bank Passbooks or Account Statements** – Especially for fixed deposits, savings accounts, or recurring deposits.
3. **Loan Agreements** – For home, vehicle, or personal loans. These will help during disputes, refinancing, or pre-closure.
4. **Insurance Policies** – Life, health, vehicle, and home insurance. Keep scanned PDFs in a cloud folder and ensure your nominee or spouse has access.
5. **Investment Proofs** – Mutual fund statements, shareholding records, SIP mandates, PPF passbooks, etc.
6. **Tax Returns** – At least the last 3 years' ITRs along with Form 16s.

7. **Property Documents** – Sale deed, electricity bills, Khata certificate, EC copies.
8. **Vehicle Documents** – RC book, insurance papers, PUC, and servicing history.
9. **Receipts for High-Value Purchases** – Phones, electronics, or gold—especially if needed for warranty or resale.

Create a folder on your cloud storage titled "Important Docs – Family." Under this, make subfolders like "ID Proofs," "Insurance," "Investments," "Loans," etc. Take clear photos or scans of each document, label them with the date and purpose, and upload them.

Once you've backed them up, verify expiry dates—especially for insurance and PUC. Then, make a printed file at home that mirrors your digital version. It's also wise to share access with a trusted family member or spouse, in case you're unreachable during emergencies.

Doing this once gives you mental peace every single month. You'll never scramble for papers again when it matters most.

Most people assume that bills are non-negotiable. That's often not true. The reality is, many of us are overpaying without realising it. Whether it's the broadband plan that's more than we need, the OTT combo pack we don't use fully, or the mobile data plans we don't consume, there's hidden leakage in every corner.

Start with your **internet bill**. Are you paying for 300 Mbps when you barely stream HD content or work with large files? Can you downgrade to a 100 Mbps plan and save ₹300 a month? That's ₹3,600 a year, just from one adjustment.

Cable or DTH services are another source of leaks. Are you paying ₹500+ every month but mostly watch content on Netflix or YouTube? Time to trim the channel pack or even consider disconnecting entirely.

Mobile plans are notorious. Most postpaid plans have bundled features like Disney+ or Amazon Prime, but are you using them? If not, consider switching to prepaid or a more basic postpaid plan. Check family plans, too. You can often combine three numbers into a cheaper single plan.

Then there are **gas and electricity bills**. Overbilling due to faulty meters or estimated readings is common. Always check your meter reading against your bill. Raise a complaint if something looks off.

A family in Surat reduced their combined household service bills from ₹5,400 to ₹3,900 by simply switching broadband providers, consolidating mobile plans, and trimming their cable subscription. That's ₹18,000 saved annually—just by paying attention.

This kind of review should become a monthly practice. Every ₹100 saved here is ₹100 that can be invested, saved, or used for something meaningful.

Food waste isn't just a kitchen problem—it's a financial problem too. Every rotting tomato, expired biscuit packet, or uneaten bowl of rice translates directly to wasted money. Chapter 4 walked you through grocery planning like a French chef, and here's where that wisdom comes full circle.

Go back to your fridge, freezer, and pantry. How much of what you bought last week has been used? Are veggies turning soggy? Are leftovers piling up uneaten? Is the bread going mouldy before the week ends?

Here's what 34-year-old Sumati from Bengaluru did: She created a "Use First" basket in her fridge. Anything that was nearing expiry or freshness went into this tray. Every dinner was planned using something from that basket. Her food waste dropped by 60%, and she saved around ₹1,500 monthly—simply by not throwing away edible food.

Also, re-evaluate your grocery quantities. Are you buying rice in bulk but forgetting about pulses? Do you buy too many snacks and neglect breakfast staples? Review your grocery bill with last week's actual consumption. The mismatch tells a story.

Food waste isn't just waste—it's emotional. We buy things with the best intentions, then feel guilt when we toss them. Financial housekeeping includes this emotional clutter. A cleaner fridge often reflects a cleaner conscience—and a healthier bank balance.

We often think clutter is a problem of space. But more often than not, it's a problem of indecision. If your cupboards are full, your shelves are messy, and your garage is chaotic, chances are your wallet is losing money too. Why? Because duplicates and hoarded items silently block new financial opportunities.

Let's take an example. In Hyderabad, a couple decided to declutter their home. They found **three unused smartphones**, a duplicate sandwich maker, an unopened mixer grinder (a wedding gift), and over 50 pieces of unused clothing with tags. After listing these items on OLX and Facebook Marketplace, they made over ₹18,000 in three weeks.

This isn't rare—it's just that most of us never look at unused items as hidden assets. Walk through your house, room by room. If you find anything you haven't used in the last six months and it still works, ask yourself: *Would someone else value this more than me?*

From duplicate headphones and blenders to unused fitness gear and power banks, every home has a pile of "not now" items that quietly become "never." Sell them while they still have resale value. If you're not sure of the price, look up similar listings and price slightly lower for a quicker sale.

Some items can even be donated for a tax deduction, especially in the case of clothes, books, and old laptops. Take photos, log the details, and ask the NGO for an acknowledgement receipt. Every step helps.

Financial housekeeping isn't just about managing money. It's also about managing *space and value*. A clutter-free home often leads to clearer priorities and more mindful purchases in the future.

Electricity is one of those monthly expenses that we accept without question. But look closer, and you'll see it's one of the easiest areas to optimise. You don't need to live in the dark or sweat through summers. You just need small, consistent energy-saving habits.

Start with **appliance timing**. Your geyser doesn't need to be on for 30 minutes. Most modern water heaters take less than 10 minutes to heat. Set a timer or use a smart plug. Similarly, turn off your modem/router when you sleep—yes, it uses power even when idle.

Switch to LED bulbs in every room. It's an investment that pays off. An average LED bulb consumes 80% less energy than an incandescent bulb and lasts longer. A middle-class household that switched 12 bulbs to LEDs saw a monthly bill drop from ₹1,800 to ₹1,400 in just two months.

Fridge maintenance also matters. Keep it 2/3rd full for efficient cooling, clean the coils every 6 months, and avoid placing hot food inside immediately. These small things reduce the compressor's workload and extend the fridge's life, too.

Another hidden saver? **Air conditioning discipline.** Keep it at 24–25°C instead of 20–22°C. Use ceiling fans to circulate air. Every 1-degree difference saves around 6% of energy. If your AC is older than 7–8 years, it may be worth checking the energy rating and upgrading.

Also consider **solar-powered outdoor lights** or motion-sensor lighting for balconies and driveways. They're affordable now and add a safety bonus, too.

By focusing on energy use, you're not just reducing your bill—you're contributing to a greener planet and freeing up funds for other priorities.

Follow the checklist below and Review the Whole House

Now that your mindset is aligned with financial housekeeping, it's time to go physical. Walk through your home, one space at a time. Use the checklist provided below. Treat it like a treasure hunt—not for gold, but for savings, safety, and sanity.

If something is broken, outdated, duplicated, or costing you extra, it gets marked. You can use a printed version, your phone notes, or an app like Notion or Google Keep.

Here's how to go about it:

Living Room

- Check the TV/set-top box for unnecessary channels or AMC (Annual Maintenance Contract) charges.
- Fan motors and blades—are they balanced and noise-free? Unbalanced fans consume more energy and cause wear.
- Look at gadgets lying around—do you still use them?
- Lighting—are you still using halogens or CFLs?
- Upholstery and curtains—need cleaning or repair?
- Any termite or pest signs behind furniture?
- Discard old newspapers and magazines—scan what's needed, recycle the rest.

Kitchen

- Chimney filters clogged? Clean or replace.
- Fridge—is the rubber lining sealing properly?
- Microwave, gas stove, induction cooktop—working efficiently?
- Is your LPG rubber pipe within the safe usage period?
- Have you tracked your gas refills lately?

- Are jars, tiffins, or blenders cracked or leaking?
- Pantry—check expiry dates and overstock.
- Is your water purifier filter due for a change?
- Do you need an LPG safety certificate?
- AC in the kitchen working well or leaking?

Bedroom

- Plug points and chargers—any sparks or loose fittings?
- Mattress due for a deep clean? Allergens build up.
- Inverter battery topped with water?
- Are bedside medicines expired?
- Old clothes piling up? Can some be donated?
- Geyser scaling—have you checked the heating speed?

Bathroom

- Taps and pipes—any slow leaks?
- Showerheads clogged or weak?
- Are the tiles or grout turning black?
- Expired first-aid items?
- Is your washing machine vibrating, making noise, or draining poorly?

Laundry Area

- Is scaling from hard water affecting machines?
- Are drying stands broken or rusted?
- Are you using too much detergent? (Check for leftover soap on clothes)
- Dhobi costs—are you outsourcing too much laundry?

- Is your vehicle due for a wash or service?

By now, you've done a deep review of your living room, kitchen, bedroom, and bathroom. But the magic of financial housekeeping lies in the details. The following areas are often overlooked—and that's why they often hide the biggest waste.

Laundry Area

It's more than just your washing machine—it's a zone where tiny inefficiencies snowball into large monthly costs.

Hard water scaling can drastically reduce your machine's life and its ability to wash properly. If you live in a city with hard water, like Chennai or parts of Delhi, using a water softener can extend your washing machine's lifespan. A ₹500 water descaler investment can save thousands in machine repairs.

Check **the broken drying stands**. If they're unstable or rusting, they're accidents waiting to happen. Replace or repair them before they collapse (possibly with your wet clothes on them). You can also check if you really need more than one stand.

Detergent overuse is an invisible cost. Many people pour freely, thinking "more soap = cleaner clothes." But too much soap wears out fabrics faster and leads to white streaks. Read your detergent's instructions—most require just one scoop for a full load.

Lastly, the **dhobi (laundry service) costs** should be examined. Are you paying for ironing shirts that you barely wear? Can you shift to alternate weeks? A woman in Mumbai reduced her monthly dhobi bill from ₹2,500 to ₹1,200 just by shifting to alternate-week pickups and air-drying shirts on hangers.

And yes, don't forget to check the **vehicle servicing** schedule—often a part of the laundry or garage area in Indian homes. If you've missed a service, it's not just about vehicle health—it could mean penalties, reduced mileage, or increased fuel expenses.

Garage

Let's roll into the garage—literally and financially. It's where money often sits idle in the form of neglected maintenance or delayed documents.

Start with **battery levels**. A weak battery often gives no warning before failing, which leads to emergency replacement, always costlier. If your battery is older than three years, get it tested at a local mechanic.

Insurance delays are a huge hidden liability. Delayed renewals can lead to penalty fees or, worse, non-coverage during accidents. Mark your vehicle insurance dates on your phone calendar with a one-week prior alert.

Also, check **the PUC (Pollution Under Control) certificate** status. It's often forgotten until you're stopped by the traffic police. Fines can go up to ₹10,000 in some states.

Now look at your **bicycle's condition**, if you own one. If it's out of use, sell it before it rusts beyond value. Or tune it up—it's a great backup for short trips.

Is your **toolkit complete**? Missing spare jacks, rusted wrenches, or flat screwdrivers can delay even basic repairs. Create a basic list of emergency tools and replace what's damaged or missing.

And finally, scan the garage for **mosquito breeding pots**—old tyres, buckets, or trays that collect water. This isn't just hygiene—it's a direct healthcare cost if someone falls sick due to dengue or malaria.

Balcony

The balcony is often a neglected part of the house, especially if it's mostly decorative. But even here, leaks in money and efficiency quietly fester.

Check for **drain clogs**. Water accumulation can lead to damp walls inside and outside. Fixing water damage later costs exponentially more.

Look at **rusted furniture**—the metal swing that no one uses or the iron chair with loose bolts. Either refurbish or remove it. Don't let it decay silently.

Outdoor lighting may seem minor, but if you use power-hungry halogens or leave lights on all night, it adds up. Replace with solar garden lights or motion sensors.

Garden tool wear is another point. Are your watering cans cracked? Hoses leaking? Fix them or consider automating your garden watering if you're someone who forgets often. Automation sounds fancy, but simple drip systems now cost less than ₹1,000.

Also, check for **old gadgets or gifts** stored in balconies due to a lack of space. Many people store unused TVs or gift boxes here. Sell or regift them—don't let dust claim their value.

Store Room

Now comes the most magical (and sometimes mythical) part of Indian homes—the storeroom. It's the "we'll use it someday" vault. But remember: every item stored has an invisible carrying cost—space, safety, and mental clutter.

Start with **expired batteries and torches**. Most batteries have a 2–3 year shelf life. Expired ones can leak and corrode the device itself.

Check **seasonal gear**—blankets, woollens, travel bags, raincoats, heaters. Are they organised? Are they still in usable condition? If you haven't used that old raincoat for 3 monsoons, you won't next year either.

Look through **old paint cans**. Paint has a shelf life of 2–3 years max once opened. Dried, separated, or mouldy paint should be discarded safely.

Stored cardboard boxes should be evaluated. Are they still needed? Can they be recycled or flattened for compact storage?

Look for **duplicate items**. Two irons? Three emergency lights? Four umbrellas? Pick the best and donate or discard the rest.

Finally, inspect for **loose switchboards or old wiring**, a major fire hazard. If anything sparks or crackles when touched, call an electrician.

Home Safety

Home safety items are rarely reviewed unless there's an incident, and that's risky, not just financially but emotionally too.

Check if you have a **fire extinguisher**. If not, this is a non-negotiable purchase. Basic kitchen models cost ₹1,000–₹2,000 and last for 5 years.

Inspect **mosquito net tears**. A torn net welcomes insects and invites medical bills. Fix or replace immediately.

Throw away **expired repellents**, especially coils and sprays. Not only do they become ineffective, but the chemicals can degrade and be harmful.

Review **locks and grills**. A jammed lock is not only frustrating but also unsafe in emergencies. Oil the hinges, test the keys, and replace faulty ones.

Check **torch batteries** and replace them. Keep one torch per bedroom. If the power goes out, you'll thank yourself.

Do you have a **smoke detector**? If not, strongly consider installing one, especially near the kitchen and bedroom corridor. They are inexpensive life savers.

Digital and Services

Last but not least is the virtual world, where more and more of our spending now happens.

Check **learning or game app subscriptions**. Many kids' apps auto-renew monthly. Ask your children or partner if they're still using them. If not, cancel.

Are you paying for **cloud storage** you don't use? Many families pay ₹130/month for 100 GB when their Google storage is only half full. Trim to 15 GB free if possible.

Review **auto-renewal apps** like yoga classes, language learning, or diet plans. Are they still part of your life or just your financial past?

Check **postpaid mobile plans**. Are you using all the data you're paying for? A friend of mine was paying ₹999 per month for a 100 GB plan when she only used 15 GB. A ₹399 plan worked just fine.

And lastly, check if you're still using **antivirus subscriptions or Microsoft Office** paid versions. With built-in Windows Defender and free alternatives like LibreOffice, many households can avoid this recurring cost.

You're now ready to conduct your very own Financial Housekeeping Audit. To make it effective, keep these tools handy:

- **A notebook or printed checklist** to note issues, due renewals, or repair requirements. Handwritten notes have the power of memory.

- **Your phone** – take pictures of broken plugs, expired items, or anything that needs to be replaced. Use a note-taking app or Google Photos album for documentation.
- **Use a highlighter** to mark urgent or high-cost items. Prioritise them over the month. For instance, a leaky gas pipe or an expired fire extinguisher is high-priority. But a rusted chair can wait.

Move room to room methodically. You can do this in 3–4 hours spread across two days, or delegate parts of the checklist to family members. Make it fun—reward yourself with a treat afterwards!

Now that you've reviewed your documents, it's time to bring it all together into one simple sheet—your Monthly Financial One-Pager. Think of this as your dashboard, a single-page summary that gives you a snapshot of your financial health at a glance. You don't need to be a finance geek or Excel wizard. You just need a page that makes sense to *you*.

Start with your income streams: salary, freelance payments, rental income, dividends—whatever applies. Then, list your fixed expenses: rent/EMI, groceries, school fees, utility bills, fuel, etc. These usually don't change much month-to-month.

Next, track your variable expenses: eating out, entertainment, shopping, medical costs, and travel. These are the categories where overspending often hides.

Also, include your savings and investments for the month. SIPs, RD/FD contributions, gold purchases, or any emergency fund top-up.

Finally, add a section for dues and reminders. This can include upcoming EMIs, premium due dates, tax filing deadlines, or any large payment expected next month.

Here's how a sample one-pager might look:

- **Income**: ₹50,000
- **Fixed Expenses**: ₹28,000
- **Variable Expenses**: ₹9,500
- **Savings/Investments**: ₹10,000
- **Balance**: ₹2,500
- **Reminders**: LIC premium on 20th, PPF contribution by 30th

You can maintain this in a diary, a Google Sheet, or even a whiteboard at home. The goal is to develop a monthly ritual around it. As you build this habit, you'll start spotting patterns—months you overspend, categories you forget to save in, or how small amounts add up.

A 28-year-old teacher named Pranav began maintaining this one-pager and, within six months, managed to save an additional ₹15,000 just by noticing repetitive restaurant spending. Awareness drives change, and this simple tool is your monthly mirror.

Financial housekeeping isn't just about trimming costs or organising bills. It's about reclaiming control. It's about not being blindsided by sudden expenses, late fees, or the slow drip of overspending.

It's about making space—not just physically, but mentally. A clean space encourages a clear mind. When your bank account is aligned, your home is organised, and your subscriptions are intentional, you create space for peace.

Think of it like self-care. Just like you brush your teeth or clean your wardrobe, your finances deserve a regular ritual. Once a month, walk through your home. Run your checklist. Review your budget. Clean your apps. Reflect on what's truly useful—and what isn't.

And here's the beauty of it: you don't need to aim for perfection. You just need to aim for awareness. When you become aware, you become powerful. You make better decisions, you feel more in control, and over time, your home and finances reflect that confidence.

So, make this a part of your monthly rhythm. Every Day 5 to 7, give your finances—and your home—a fresh breath of air. Because in the end, financial housekeeping isn't just about saving money. It's about building a life that feels less chaotic and more intentional.

☑ Key Takeaways From This Chapter

- Financial housekeeping is about **decluttering money habits**, not mops and brooms.
- A **Day 5–7 review** helps catch overspending early and course-correct.
- Setting **spending limits** via apps and cards builds financial discipline.
- Regular **auto-debit audits** prevent silent money leaks.

- Reviewing **subscriptions** avoids "death by ₹199 cuts."
- Closing **dormant accounts and unused credit lines** reduces clutter and risk.
- Negotiating **loan rates and insurance premiums** saves thousands annually.
- A **bill and receipt filing system** reduces stress and tax-time chaos.
- Backing up **essential financial documents** ensures quick access in emergencies.
- Reviewing **utility bills** prevents overpayment for services not used.
- Tackling **food waste** directly saves money and guilt.
- Decluttering **duplicate gadgets and unused items** creates hidden income.
- Smart **energy use** lowers electricity bills and extends appliance life.
- A **room-by-room financial checklist** uncovers hidden costs at home.
- A **Monthly One-Pager** simplifies tracking income, expenses, and reminders.
- Financial housekeeping is **self-care for your wallet and mind**.

✍ Exercises for You

1. Walk around your home with a notebook and mark at least 5 financial leaks (unused subscriptions, duplicate gadgets, overdue bills). Write the corrective action beside each.

2. Involve your family. Whoever finds the most expired, unused, or wasteful items wins a reward.
3. Withdraw a fixed cash amount for discretionary spending this week. Physically handle and track every rupee.
4. File and scan 3 important documents today (PAN, Aadhaar, Insurance policy). Store them digitally and share access with a trusted family member.
5. Cancel or pause one subscription today, and note how it impacts your lifestyle for a week.

CHAPTER 6

GAME ON (DAYS 8 AND 9)

Saving Through Fun, Discipline, and Micro-Experiments

Purpose of the Chapter:

To introduce short-term money challenges that motivate savings and discipline through creativity, playfulness, and community. This chapter shows how to gamify saving and reduce boredom around budgets.

What You'll Learn in This Chapter:

- Monthly saving challenges that work even with low income
- How small restrictions build lifelong financial muscles
- Turning saving into a dopamine-triggering habit
- Involving friends, partners, or social media for accountability
- Examples of real people saving big through small challenges

"Every rupee saved in a challenge becomes a trophy you never forget."

CHAPTER VI

GAME ON (DAYS 8 AND 9)

> *Gamification is not about turning life into a game, but about borrowing the best elements of games to make life more engaging.*

Suppose you've ever watched a reality TV game show. In that case, you'll know that nothing makes people more determined than a little bit of competition and a clock ticking in the background. There's a certain thrill in completing a challenge, proving to yourself that you can go without something, resist temptation, or build something new from scratch. Now imagine taking that same excitement and applying it to your monthly budget. Sound ridiculous? Trust me—it's not. In fact, it might be the most fun you've ever had with your money.

Challenges aren't just for gym freaks or puzzle lovers. When it comes to managing your salary, especially if you're living month-to-month, gamifying your money habits can make budgeting feel less like a punishment and more like an adventure. It's a clever psychological trick. You take a typically dull task—saving money or reducing expenses—and dress it up in challenge form with rules, goals, and even small rewards. Suddenly, what used to feel like financial handcuffs becomes a game you're excited to play. Whether it's a no-spend day or squeezing a week's groceries into ₹1000, each challenge brings a unique way to shake up the monotony and give your wallet a breather.

This chapter is a buffet of such challenges. From tried-and-tested classics like the No-Spend Week to quirkier ones like the ₹10 Jar Game, there's something in here for everyone. Pick one, try it, tweak it, repeat it, and most importantly—learn from it. You'll start noticing which habits drain your bank account the most, where your self-control shines, and where you might need a bit more structure. Ready to play? Let's dive into the challenge zone.

1. The 7-Day No-Spend Challenge: Zero is the New Hero

Let's start with the ultimate classic: the No-Spend Challenge. The idea is simple but powerful—don't spend any money for seven straight days, except for absolute necessities like transport to work, medicine, or an emergency recharge. That means no online orders, no quick snacks from Swiggy, no chai from the tapri, and definitely no late-night retail therapy. If it's not essential, it doesn't get a rupee.

> ***Pro-tip:*** *Before starting, remove your saved cards from shopping apps. It reduces temptation instantly.*

This challenge is more than just a money-saving tactic—it's a mirror that shows you your unconscious habits. That mindless

₹200 on a cab you could've avoided, or the ₹60 chai every day that adds up to ₹1800 a month—it all becomes crystal clear. You start using what's in your kitchen. You rediscover the joy of home-cooked food. You walk instead of booking an auto. It may sound tough, but the benefits are substantial.

Take Shweta, a 28-year-old content writer in Pune. She tried the 7-day no-spend challenge after realising her monthly budget was going off-track. By the end of the week, she'd saved ₹2,500 without feeling deprived. "It was like financial yoga," she laughed. "Uncomfortable at first, but super satisfying in the end."

So, if you've never tried a challenge before, start here. Zero might just be your new favourite number.

2. The ₹1000 Grocery Budget Challenge: MasterChef, Budget Edition

Here's a spicy one for the foodies: cook all your meals for one week with just ₹1000. Sounds impossible? Well, that's the point. This challenge forces you to plan every bite you eat, make friends with local vendors, and reimagine your pantry as a treasure chest of hidden ingredients.

The trick lies in three things—smart planning, simple meals, and embracing the humble power of vegetables and grains. You'll find that lentils, rice, poha, and seasonal vegetables can stretch a long way. Add in a little spice magic and suddenly you're having dal fry, aloo bhaji, veg pulao, and poha upma without spending more than ₹150 a day.

Meet Rachit and Simran, a newly married couple in Mumbai. They tried this challenge to balance their wedding-related spending. They started with a handwritten list, stuck to buying from street vendors instead of supermarkets, and cooked all their meals at home—even their Sunday brunch. "We got creative," Rachit said. "Simran made a beetroot pulao that was weirdly amazing."

Not only did they meet the ₹1000 goal, but they also discovered how much money was leaking from their Swiggy and Zomato orders before. Give this challenge a go—and who knows, you might walk out of it with better health and more money.

3. The "Use What You Have" Month: The Anti-Amazon Experiment

Raise your hand if you've ordered something online, only to realise you already had a version of it lying somewhere at home. We're all guilty. That's why this next challenge is all about restraint—and reinvention. For one whole month, commit to using only what you already own. No new clothes. No new gadgets. No pantry restocks unless something truly runs out. Your mission? Get creative with what you've got.

This isn't just a budgeting exercise—it's also an exploration into the forgotten corners of your fridge, wardrobe, bookshelf, and makeup drawer. It's the month when you turn old kurtas into loungewear, leftover rice into crispy patties, and extra shampoo samples into your main bathroom stash.

One participant, Rohini from Nagpur, chronicled her journey in a blog post titled "A Month Without Amazon."

She wore clothes she hadn't touched in years, baked her own birthday cake, and even DIY-ed a broken shelf. "I thought I'd feel restricted," she wrote. "Instead, I felt like a resourceful genius."

You'll be amazed at how much you already have. The real treasure isn't on Flipkart—it's probably in the second drawer of your kitchen.

4. The 30-Day Cash-Only Challenge: Swipe No More

We live in a world where the click of a button can cost you money. A tap here, a swipe there—and boom, your budget takes a silent hit. That's exactly why the Cash-Only Challenge exists: to bring back visibility, accountability, and a tangible connection with your spending.

Here's the deal—you withdraw a fixed amount of money at the beginning of the week or month and commit to using *only* that cash for all expenses. No UPI, no debit cards, no credit cards. If you run out, you pause spending. It forces discipline in a way digital transactions simply can't.

People often report that paying in cash feels more "real." There's something about physically handing over a ₹500 note that stings just a little more than a tap on your phone. You hesitate, consider alternatives, and end up making better choices.

Siddharth, a marketing executive in Bangalore, tried this for 30 days. He kept a simple pocket diary and noted down every expense. He cut down his impulse buying by 40% just because seeing his cash deplete physically was a reminder to slow down.

"The urge to grab a coffee just because I passed a café? Gone," he said. "I started making coffee at work."

The cash-only challenge doesn't just save you money—it sharpens your decision-making skills. And when you're forced to "budget by feel," you'll be surprised how much more thoughtful you become.

5. The 1% Daily Savings Challenge: Small Drops, Big Pond

This one is all about tiny, consistent effort that builds into something meaningful. Save just 1% of your daily income every day for 30 days. Let's say you earn ₹50,000 a month, that's around ₹1,667 a day. One per cent of that is just ₹16.67—less than a cup of chai.

> ***Pro-tip:*** *Automate this by setting up a daily bank auto-transfer into a* ***liquid mutual fund or gold****. There are apps to do that.*

Put that amount away—physically in a jar or digitally into a savings wallet—*every single day*. You can even use stickers or a tracking chart to stay motivated. It's a micro habit, but it makes a macro difference. At the end of the month, you'll have saved around ₹500—and more importantly, you'll have trained your brain to associate daily routine with saving.

A surprising number of people find this challenge the easiest to start with. Anjali, a teacher in Delhi, stuck to it for two months and saved ₹1000+ without blinking. "It's so little I barely noticed," she laughed, "but watching my tracker fill up was weirdly satisfying."

This isn't about the amount—it's about the muscle. Saving ₹16 might not feel powerful, but doing it daily gives you discipline, awareness, and momentum. And once you start enjoying the act, you'll likely want to increase that number.

6. The Subscription Detox: Press Pause on the Leaks

We're living in a world of silent, automatic subscriptions. OTT platforms, cloud storage, gym memberships, music streaming, and paid apps—quietly nibble at your bank balance. That's where the Subscription Detox Challenge comes in.

The goal? For 30 days, cancel or pause every non-essential subscription. Ask yourself: Am I *actually* using Netflix enough to justify it? Is that fitness app motivating me—or do I just feel guilty every time it charges me?

You don't have to go cold turkey. Start with a list of all your subscriptions—check your email or bank statement if needed. Then, evaluate them brutally. Pause them. Replace them with free versions if possible. Watch YouTube instead of Netflix. Use free audiobooks from the library instead of Audible. Try home workouts on Instagram instead of a pricey fitness app.

Ravi, a freelance designer from Kochi, saved over ₹1800 during his subscription detox month. "I realized I hadn't logged into half of them for weeks," he said. "I didn't miss them—except my Spotify playlist. That one I brought back."

This challenge helps you plug the leaks you forgot existed. And once you're done, you'll never blindly hit "renew" again.

7. ₹10 Savings Jar Game: The Joy of Tiny Penalties

Sometimes the best way to discipline yourself is to make it fun. The ₹10 Savings Jar Game is a playful but powerful challenge. Every time you break a rule—ordering food, skipping a packed lunch, shopping online—you drop ₹10 or ₹20 into a jar. Think of it like a "naughty tax."

It's not about punishing yourself—it's about turning awareness into a habit. The jar becomes your scoreboard. Watching the money pile up becomes oddly satisfying. You begin noticing patterns—like how often you order to skip cooking, or cave into random expenses.

> ***Pro-tip:*** *Keep the jar visible in your living room—it acts as a daily reminder of your progress.*

You can also flip the game—reward yourself with ₹10 every time you *resist* temptation. Did you skip the fancy coffee? Add ₹10. Did you walk instead of booking a cab? Add ₹20. Suddenly, you're training your brain to feel rewarded for good choices.

Chitra, a single mom in Hyderabad, turned this into a family game. "My son even started reminding me—'Mummy, you skipped dinner outside, add ten rupees!'" she laughed. By the end of the month, their jar had ₹640—and a bunch of new habits.

Whether it's coins in a jar or transfers to a savings wallet, the principle remains the same—gamify your discipline, and it'll never feel like a punishment.

8. The "Don't Break the Chain" Challenge: Habit Makes the Hero

There's a popular productivity hack that says: once you start a streak, don't break it. Every day you succeed at your habit, you mark an X on the calendar. Over time, your motivation isn't just to save—it's to keep the chain going. This method works brilliantly for saving money.

Pick one money-saving habit—bringing lunch to work, skipping your daily chai, cooking dinner—and do it daily for 30 days. Each day you succeed, mark it on a big, visible calendar. Your goal? Don't break the chain.

As the days go by, your motivation shifts. You no longer just want to save money—you want that long, beautiful chain of Xs to continue. It becomes a game you play with yourself. Break it once, and you'll feel it. Keep it going, and it's addictive in the best way.

Karan, a junior architect in Jaipur, used this to build the lunch-packing habit. He stuck his calendar on the fridge. "After 11 days, I didn't want to stop," he said. "I even woke up 20 minutes earlier to cook when I was late. The Xs had taken over my brain!"

Sometimes, it's not about money—it's about the momentum. Start your chain. Don't break it.

9. The Social Spending Fast: Friends Without Finances

We often underestimate how much we spend just to be social—movie tickets, café meetups, mall visits, bar nights. But here's the truth: connection doesn't need cash. This challenge dares you to go one week—or a full month—without *any* social spending.

Sounds scary? It shouldn't. It's an invitation to be creative. Instead of brunch at a fancy café, how about a potluck at someone's home? Swap that movie ticket for a game night. Go for a morning walk instead of a breakfast date. Host a terrace picnic, complete with home-cooked food and a Bluetooth speaker.

Nisha, a social butterfly in Ahmedabad, did this for 30 days and chronicled it on Instagram. "At first, my friends laughed," she said. "But then they joined in. We had themed nights at home, free museum visits, and dance parties in our living rooms."

Not only did she save ₹6,000 that month, but she also felt more connected than ever. "The distractions went away—we actually talked," she said.

Try it, and you might find your most valuable connections don't need a bill at the end.

10. The Reverse Budget Day: Flip the Script

We usually budget by planning what we'll spend. But what if, for one day, you did the exact opposite? Welcome to the Reverse Budget Day Challenge. The goal is simple yet radical: spend absolutely nothing for one full day—not even for essentials. Instead, challenge yourself to survive using only what you already have.

Start by scanning your kitchen. What leftovers or neglected ingredients can become your meals for the day? Next, think about your travel. Can you walk, cycle, or carpool? What about entertainment? Can you read a book you already own, or watch a free YouTube documentary?

It's like a 24-hour "financial fast." You become hyper-aware of how many things you *usually* pay for automatically—and how often they're not really necessary.

Vikram, a startup co-founder from Pune, tried this on a lazy Sunday. He wrote in his journal, "No Zomato. No Amazon. No petrol. I walked to the local park with a sandwich from home. It was oddly peaceful. I realised how much I lean on money to 'fix' boredom."

Try doing this once every fortnight. Over time, you'll not only reduce expenses but also improve your resourcefulness and mindfulness. And when money stops being the default solution, creativity flows in.

11. The Dream Goal Savings Challenge: Budgeting for Joy

Budgeting often feels like a list of "nos"—no eating out, no new clothes, no fun. But what if you flipped it into a yes? That's what the Dream Goal Savings Challenge is about. Pick one exciting, feel-good dream—maybe a trip to Manali, a new phone, or a painting for your wall—and start saving *specifically* for it.

> ***Pro-tip:*** *Add visuals. Print a picture of your dream trip, phone, or goal and stick it on your fridge.*

Let's say your goal costs ₹10,000. Break it down: ₹2500 per week for a month, or ₹333 per day for 30 days. Set a visual tracker—a thermometer chart, a puzzle where each piece equals ₹500, or even an envelope system. As you hit milestones, give yourself tiny non-spending rewards—a night off chores, a homemade spa day, or a movie from your collection.

Disha, a 34-year-old school teacher in Nashik, used this challenge to save for a solo vacation. "Saving felt like feeding my dream, not punishing my fun," she said. "Every ₹100 I added to my envelope felt like packing a pair of socks for the trip."

By aligning budgeting with joy, you change the narrative. It's no longer about lack—it's about *preparation* for something wonderful.

12. The "Zero-Waste Money Week" Challenge: Nothing Wasted, Everything Gained

This is one of the most mindful challenges on the list. For one full week, make sure nothing you *buy* goes to waste—whether it's food, water, electricity, or even the shampoo you use. It's not just about frugality—it's about respect. Respect for resources, for effort, and yes, for money.

So how do you begin? Start by finishing everything edible in your fridge before cooking something new. Use leftovers to make new dishes. Time your mobile charging so it doesn't overheat and waste electricity. Use every last bit of that shampoo before opening a new bottle. Fix broken items before replacing them.

Tanvi, a sustainability blogger from Goa, took on this challenge and shared her hacks on Instagram. She made vegetable stock from peels, charged her devices only when needed, finished all half-used condiments, and even repaired old clothes. "I saved over ₹900 without even trying," she said. "But more than that, I felt proud. Proud of not being wasteful."

The money saved here often sneaks up on you—it's not loud like a cancelled subscription, but it's constant. And the environmental karma? That's a bonus worth its weight in gold.

13. Create Your Own Personal Challenge: Tailor-Made Discipline

Nobody knows your worst money habit better than you do. Maybe it's ordering food at midnight. Maybe it's those endless Insta impulse buys. Or maybe you're always late paying bills, and you rack up late fees. Whatever it is, you now have the power to create a challenge that targets it—personally.

> ***Pro-tip:*** *Involve an accountability partner—it doubles your success rate.*

Step one: Identify your financial kryptonite. Step two: Set your own rules. Maybe you'll go 14 days without ordering online. Or vow to pay every bill on the first of the month, no exceptions. Step three: Set a tiny reward. It could be guilt-free screen time, a special home-cooked meal, or a coffee date with yourself.

This works even better if you involve someone else. Tell a friend about your challenge. Or better, challenge them to do it too. You both become accountability partners. Share progress, setbacks, and wins.

Aarav and his college roommate did this with food delivery. They created a 15-day "No Swiggy Pact" with ₹100 penalties paid to the other person for every violation. By the end of two weeks, not only had they saved over ₹1800 each, but they had started cooking together, which became a whole new bonding ritual.

Make your challenge. Own your rules. Customise your self-discipline.

Conclusion: Turning Challenges into Change

Here's the thing about challenges: at first, they seem like tiny obstacles. But give them time, and they become powerful teachers. Each one nudges you toward better decisions, stronger habits, and a clearer understanding of what matters most.

From no-spend weeks to cash-only months, every challenge in this chapter is a tiny laboratory of change. They aren't meant to be permanent. They're not punishments. They're invitations to play—with purpose. They reveal things about your habits, your impulses, your strengths, and your resilience.

What matters most is *consistency*. You don't need to do every challenge every month. But imagine picking *just one* challenge each month for a year. That's twelve new financial muscles you've trained. That's twelve opportunities to see your money differently. To save, spend, and plan better—not from fear, but from awareness.

And don't forget to celebrate the wins—no matter how small. Did you make it through a week of no spending? High-five yourself. Completed a ₹10 Jar Game and filled it? Do a happy dance. Manage to avoid Swiggy for a fortnight? You're a legend. These are victories that build your financial story.

So don't wait for motivation. Don't wait for a big salary bump or a life crisis to start thinking about money. Start with a challenge. Build your own momentum.

You've played games before. Now it's time to win the one that matters most—your own financial growth.

Game on.

☑ Key Takeaways From This Chapter

- **No-Spend Challenge** – Save big by avoiding all non-essential spending for a week.
- **₹1000 Grocery Challenge** – Cook every meal for a week with just ₹1000.
- **Use What You Have Month** – Survive using only what's already at home.
- **Cash-Only Challenge** – Spend only with cash to increase awareness and control.
- **1% Daily Savings Challenge** – Save 1% of daily income to build lasting discipline.
- **Subscription Detox** – Pause unused subscriptions to stop silent money leaks.
- **₹10 Savings Jar Game** – Add money as a penalty or reward to gamify discipline.
- **Don't Break the Chain** – Build savings habits with streaks and consistency.

- **Social Spending Fast** – Replace costly outings with free, creative activities.
- **Reverse Budget Day** – Spend nothing for a day to boost resourcefulness.
- **Dream Goal Savings Challenge** – Save with joy toward a personal goal.
- **Zero-Waste Money Week** – Ensure nothing you buy goes to waste.
- **Personal Challenge** – Create customised rules to target your weak money habits.

Exercises for You

1. Take a blank calendar and mark your chosen challenge days with a ☑ as you complete them.
2. Create a **₹10 Jar** and physically drop coins whenever you spend unnecessarily or resist temptation.
3. Do a kitchen inventory exercise, list 10 meals you can make with only what you already have.
4. Set up three envelopes (Food, Travel, Fun) and use only cash for a week. Track how you felt each day.
5. Print or draw your dream goal tracker (like a thermometer chart) and colour it in as you save.

CHAPTER 7

MID-MONTH RESET (DAY 10 TO 13)

Realigning Your Budget Before It's Too Late

Purpose of the Chapter:

To teach the importance of pausing mid-month to assess how the budget is holding up against real life. It's a checkpoint—not a punishment—designed to realign, re-energise, and redirect finances before habits spiral.

What You'll Learn in This Chapter:

- Conducting a mid-month audit with empathy and insight
- How to shift leftover funds toward goals, not temptations
- Fixing overspending mistakes without guilt
- Communicating financial adjustments with family or partners
- Mental clarity gained from intentional reviews

"A mid-month reset can save your entire financial month."

CHAPTER VII

MID-MONTH RESET (DAY 10 TO 13)

A journey without pauses leads to exhaustion; a budget without checkpoints leads to chaos. Stop midway, and you'll go further with strength and clarity.

Imagine driving from Mumbai to Goa. You don't wait until you're out of fuel in the middle of nowhere to check your car's status. You stop at a halfway point, refuel, check the tyres, maybe grab a vada pav, and adjust your route if needed. That's what a mid-month budget reset is — a pit stop. The 15th of every month isn't just a date; it's a golden opportunity to pause, assess, and course-correct. It's not meant to stress you out, but to strengthen your control over your finances before it's too late.

Mid-month budgeting is that underrated yet powerful checkpoint that can transform how you manage money. By this time, the buzz of payday has settled, initial bills are paid, grocery trips are made, and some spending choices have already started to show results. It's the perfect moment to stop and ask: Is my plan still working? What's veering off track? What can I fix before it snowballs?

This chapter is your toolbox. We'll walk through practical, non-intimidating methods to review your finances mid-way. You'll learn how to spot silent leaks, rebalance without guilt, prepare for the rest of the month, and even get inspired to tweak your habits for the next month. Think of it like an honest, kind, and helpful conversation with your future self. Let's make these four days, Day 10 to 13, the most important part of your money month.

Something is calming about pausing. Before you open your expense tracker or your budgeting app, pause. Make a cup of chai or coffee. Sit in your favourite corner. Pull out your notebook or journaling app. This is not an audit; this is a ritual. A mid-month ritual that gives you clarity and compassion in equal measure.

Reflection isn't about scolding yourself for spending too much on coffee. It's about listening. Three questions guide this process: What's working? What's not? What surprised me?

Maybe your decision to carry home-cooked lunch helped you save Rs. 800. That's working. Maybe your online shopping habit reared its head again. That's not working. Maybe you forgot your car insurance was due and had to dip into your emergency fund. That's surprising. Write these things down. Not to punish yourself, but to understand yourself. Take 15 to 20 minutes and simply write: no filters, no judgments. Just you, your thoughts, and your real-life spending. You'd be amazed at how much clarity a simple journaling session can bring. One reader, Ruchi from Pune, shared how she saved Rs. 5,000 in a month just by recognising her impulse Swiggy orders during stress-filled workdays. She replaced them with pre-planned snack boxes. The change started from a single written reflection.

> ***Pro-tip***: *Always journal with examples, not just numbers. Writing down real situations makes it easier to spot patterns in your spending habits.*

The 15-minute budget health scan. Think of this like a financial health checkup. Every mid-month review should include a 15-minute budget scan across four vital areas: Bills, Essentials, Fun, and Savings. You don't need fancy tools — just your digital tracker or even a simple notebook.

Go category by category. Have all your bills been paid? Any reminders from your electricity board or mobile provider? For Essentials, are groceries and medicines within range or have you been splurging on premium biscuits again? In the Fun category, are you sticking to your monthly allowance or have movie nights and spontaneous plans taken over? And most importantly, are you saving as per plan, or has that money quietly disappeared into impulse buys?

Use a colour-coded system: Green means on track, Yellow is a mild warning, Red means urgent attention. So, if your "Essentials" are 80% used but you still have half the month left, that's Red. If you've used only 20% of your Fun Money — that's Green.

Rajat from Indore began this system three months ago. He now uses Google Sheets with simple conditional formatting. Every 15th, he sits down, checks his categories, and assigns colours. His biggest win? He prevented an EMI default by catching it two days before the due date in one of his yellow alerts.

The envelope method isn't just for your grandparents. It's one of the most effective ways to stay disciplined. Whether you use physical cash envelopes or digital categories on an app like Walnut or Goodbudget, a mid-month envelope audit can be a game-changer. Let's say you had Rs. 6,000 for groceries, Rs. 2,000 for outings, and Rs. 1,000 for shopping. By Day 13, you should ideally have a healthy balance in each. But if you find your grocery envelope nearly empty while your outing budget is untouched, you need to pivot.

This audit lets you see which envelopes are bleeding and which are bloated. If groceries are running low, maybe you've over-relied on Swiggy. Maybe a surprise dinner guest costs more than you expected. Decide whether to refill, freeze, or adjust.

Take the case of Deepa, a single mom from Nagpur. She realised halfway through February that her grocery envelope was almost dry. Instead of panicking, she shifted Rs. 1,000 from her "Family Outings" envelope and challenged herself to meal prep creatively for the rest of the month. She called it her "Masala Survival Week." Not only did she survive, but she also discovered five new low-cost recipes.

There's a strange shame we attach to rebalancing our budgets mid-month. As if moving money around is a sign of failure. But think of it like rebooking your Ola cab to a better route — it's smart, not weak. Life doesn't happen in neat packages. Maybe your child's school asked for an unexpected field trip fee. Or your two-wheeler needed a sudden tyre replacement. It's okay. Rebalancing is a strategy, not defeat.

But to avoid chaos, use a rule: **Two Shifts Max.** Don't allow more than two fund reallocations per month unless it's a genuine emergency. This helps maintain discipline and prevents abuse of flexibility.

Rebalancing also helps build adaptability. For instance, Anirudh had set aside Rs. 3,000 for gym sessions, but an old injury flared up. Instead of wasting that fund, he split it — Rs. 1,500 for online physiotherapy videos and Rs. 1,500 into his "Emergency Fund." His budget stayed whole, and his body felt better, too. Give yourself the freedom to adapt. Just do it mindfully, and not as a panic reaction.

It's never the big purchases. It's the Rs. 99 subscriptions. The Rs. 49 app upgrades. The late-night Rs. 180 dessert cravings on Zomato. These tiny, sneaky spenders drain your budget quietly, like a leaky tap. Mid-month is the perfect time to run a "transaction audit." Open your SMS inbox, UPI notifications, or check your bank's monthly statement. Go line by line. Ask: Was this necessary? Was this expected?

Create a "Leak Log" where you list such micro-spends. For example, Priya found Rs. 2,300 worth of "leaks" in one month — an Amazon Kindle subscription she forgot to cancel, repeated Rs. 120 spends on snacks, and auto-renewed YouTube Premium. She cancelled three subscriptions and put a Rs. 100 snack limit per week going forward. These aren't lifestyle killers. These are budget beautifiers. Plugging leaks isn't about cutting joy. It's about buying peace of mind with every rupee saved.

Feeling out of control? Hit the reset button with a No-Spend Challenge. For 3 to 5 days, commit to zero spending — no dining out, no online purchases, no add-ons. You'll be surprised how clarifying it is. But don't walk into it blind. Plan your meals, pack your lunch, fill your vehicle tank, and make a short list of emergency allowances (like medicine).

One Bangalore-based reader, Manasvi, turned this into a fun family game. She, her husband, and two kids did a 5-day No-Spend Challenge. They batch-cooked meals, rediscovered board games, and swapped outings for terrace picnics. The reward? They saved Rs. 4,800 in five days — and used it for a monsoon weekend getaway.

To make it even more exciting, design a creative reward — a guilt-free dessert, a movie night, or that new book you've been eyeing. A no-spend phase isn't about suffering; it's about recalibration and joy.

Mid-month is a smart time to look ahead. Because what's coming up will decide what you should do now. A surprise birthday party, your child's school fees, your scooter's annual servicing, or even a religious festival — these can creep up and derail a budget. Create a visual calendar or use a digital one like Google Calendar. Mark the dates where expenses are likely. Use different colours or emojis — blue for school, red for bills, green for personal fun, yellow for uncertain or possible spending.

> ***Pro-tip**: Automate at least one small savings transfer mid-month. Even Rs. 500 can build momentum and reduce pressure at month-end.*

Let's take the case of Sameer from Jaipur. He used to constantly run into cash shortages in the last week of every month. When he began marking key events — family gatherings, puja samagri needs, friends' weddings — he found the problem wasn't overspending, it was under-anticipating. A simple shift to looking two weeks ahead saved him from borrowing money or cutting into savings.

Your future is not unpredictable. You just need to train your eyes to spot what's coming. Once you see the road ahead, you can steer better today.

Money is never just numbers. It's feelings with rupee signs. We spend when we're bored. We splurge when we're sad. We celebrate with our wallets and mourn with Amazon carts.

A mid-month check on your emotional spending is vital. Were you spending to cope? Were those midnight food deliveries a result of loneliness? Was that expensive kurti really necessary — or did you just want a small win during a bad day? This is not about guilt. It's about awareness. During your reflection phase, make a list of emotional triggers and how they connected to certain spends. Then think of replacements. Next time stress knocks, go for a walk. Call a friend. Paint. Bake. Journal. Watch a comfort movie instead of swiping your debit card.

> ***Pro-tip***: *Make it fun! Turn your No-Spend Days into theme nights, Board Game Tuesday or Home Theatre Friday. It keeps the family engaged.*

One powerful story comes from Kavita, a graphic designer from Hyderabad. She used to buy skincare products every time she had a tough client interaction. It gave her a temporary feeling of control. During a mid-month audit, she realised this pattern and made a new rule: tough day = 20-minute art sketch instead. Not only did she save Rs. 3,000/month, but she also created a mini art portfolio in three months.

Make your emotions your allies, not your debt creators.

Savings is your financial thermometer. If it's too low, the body of your budget is sick. If it's healthy, you're thriving. Mid-month is when you take the thermometer out. Measure how much you've saved so far. Check against your target. Are you 50% done with savings and halfway through the month? Great! Are you at 20% and the month is nearly over? Time to act.

Quick wins help. Try things like:

- Meal prepping for the next 7 days to avoid outside food.
- Taking the metro instead of Ola/Uber twice a week.
- Pausing all non-essential app purchases.
- Selling an unused item lying at home.

Gaurav, a techie in Bengaluru, realised on the 13th that he had saved only Rs. 1,200 out of his Rs. 5,000 goal. He cut out weekend Zomato orders, skipped café lattes, and took up a two-day data-cleaning freelance gig for Rs. 2,000. By month-end, he was at Rs. 5,800 — ahead of his target! Savings isn't just what you set aside on Day 1. It's what you fight for throughout the month.

A budget not reviewed is a lesson not learned. Each month teaches us something — if we're paying attention. Use this reset phase to take notes for the next month. Did you underestimate your electricity bill? Did your grocery budget fall short again? Did you forget an EMI?

Update your budget template with these learnings. Add new categories if needed. Increase amounts where needed. Shrink where overspending didn't bring real value.

Start a "Budget Hack" list — little tricks that worked this month. For instance:

- "Don't go to the supermarket hungry."
- "Switch to bi-weekly vegetable market runs instead of weekly."
- "Set a Swiggy budget and uninstall the app after hitting it."

These aren't just notes. They are armour for the next battle. With every tweak, you make next month easier, lighter, and smarter.

By now, you might be wondering — why don't more people talk about this? Because mid-month reviews feel optional. Until you do it once and realise, they're essential. These four days, Day 10 to 13, can change your financial game. You're not just reacting. You're preparing. You're not panicking on Day 25. You're steering on Day 15. You're not scrambling to fix things when it's too late.

You're adjusting early. This habit, when done monthly, becomes a quiet superpower. It builds awareness, resilience, and peace. And it takes less than an hour — split across a few days — to do it.

Meet Sneha and Ramesh, a couple from Kochi. They once started doing mid-month resets every 13th of the month with their filter coffee ritual. In six months, they went from arguing over money to enjoying surplus funds, investing more, and even planning their Goa vacation — completely debt-free. It wasn't magic. It was the result of a simple, consistent pause to reflect, realign, and reset.

So, here's your challenge. Mark your calendar. Make it sacred. Whether it's a tea ritual, a colourful spreadsheet, or a cosy notebook moment — make your mid-month check-in non-negotiable.

Because money is not just what you earn, it is what you understand.

☑ Key Takeaways From This Chapter

- **Mid-month reset is a pit stop** to review, refuel, and realign your money plan.
- **Reflection journaling** helps identify what's working, what's not, and what surprised you.
- **15-minute budget scan** across Bills, Essentials, Fun, and Savings keeps spending balanced.
- **Envelope method audit** highlights where money is draining and where it's left idle.

- **Rebalancing with Two Shifts Max** builds flexibility without losing discipline.
- **Transaction audit** catches sneaky leaks like small subscriptions and impulse spends.
- **No-Spend Challenge** resets habits and makes saving fun.
- **planning** prevents last-minute budget derailments by spotting upcoming expenses.
- **Emotional spending check** turns feelings into awareness instead of debt.
- **Savings thermometer check** ensures you're on track toward financial goals.
- **Quick wins like meal prep, metro rides, and decluttering** boost mid-month savings.
- **Budget hack list** helps carry forward practical lessons into next month.
- **Consistent mid-month resets** reduce stress, increase awareness, and build resilience.

✍ Exercises for You

1. Take your actual expenses from this month and manually colour-code them on paper (Green/Yellow/Red). This physical act cements the awareness.
2. Take 3 envelopes, label them Groceries, Fun, and Savings. Put mock money (or paper slips) in them as per your budget. Shuffle halfway and rebalance based on new situations.
3. For one day, act as if you're in a No-Spend Challenge. Physically cross off each avoided expense from a checklist.

4. Print a blank calendar. Each time you feel tempted to spend emotionally, mark the emotion with a symbol (e.g., for stress, for sadness). At the end of the week, review patterns.
5. Create a jar at home. Every time you save by saying no to an expense, drop a small coin or note in it. The weight of the jar becomes your reward.

CHAPTER 8

YOU SAVED IT, NOW PROTECT IT (DAYS 14 AND 15)

Shielding Your Money from Emergencies, Habits, and People

Purpose of the Chapter:

To emphasise the importance of **protecting** what's saved. It's not enough to save money—one must learn how to shield it from emotional spending, emergencies, peer pressure, and even their own impulses.

What You'll Learn in This Chapter:

- How to separate savings from spending accounts
- Emergency fund basics and how to fortify them
- Teaching yourself delayed gratification through barriers
- Understanding financial boundaries with friends and family
- How insurance, automation, and psychology help guard money

"Money you protect is money you keep. Saving is the first step. Guarding is the final one."

CHAPTER VIII

YOU SAVED IT, NOW PROTECT IT (DAYS 14 AND 15)

Someone is sitting in the shade today because someone planted a tree a long time ago.

Saving money feels like crossing the finish line. You worked hard, budgeted wisely, and sacrificed a few wants, finally seeing the balance grow. It's a satisfying moment. But what many people forget is this: saving is only half the story. What happens after you save money is just as important—maybe even more. Protection is the unsung hero of financial wisdom.

Think of your money like a home. Earning it is like building it brick by brick. Saving is like locking the door. But protecting it? That's your security system, your fire insurance, your neighbourhood watch. It's everything that ensures no unexpected disaster knocks it down. Let's introduce the three layers of financial protection that this chapter will cover: Security, Stability, and Survivability.

1. Security is about shielding your money from direct threats—frauds, scams, identity theft, and even your impulses.
2. Stability is ensuring that even if life throws curveballs—health issues, job loss, or economic downturns—your financial base stays solid.
3. Survivability is planning for your family, your future self, and your legacy—so your money lives beyond you.

We'll take you through tools that are both traditional and modern, ranging from life insurance to cybersecurity, from gold to cryptocurrency, and from Wills to automation tricks. Let's begin with a real-life cautionary tale.

Meet the Sharmas, a family of five living in Mumbai. Mr Sharma was a successful entrepreneur, and over 15 years, he built assets worth crores—real estate, mutual funds, a luxury car, and gold jewellery. But one thing he never prioritised was protection. He had minimal insurance, no written Will, and most financial information was in his head. When he passed away suddenly due to a heart attack, chaos unfolded. His wife had no idea about the investments. The children were young. There was no nominee on key accounts. A few online frauds went unnoticed, and eventually, a court case over a disputed property drained their energy and money. Within three years, the Sharma family lost almost half of their wealth—not because they didn't save, but because they didn't protect. This chapter is about making sure your story goes differently.

Insurance is not an investment. It is protection. This single distinction changes everything. Let's start with the four types of insurance every family should seriously consider: life, health, motor, and home.

Life insurance, particularly a term plan, is the cornerstone of financial protection for anyone with dependents. Imagine this: you're the primary breadwinner, and something happens to you. A term insurance payout ensures your family doesn't face a financial tsunami after dealing with the emotional one. A 1 crore term plan can cost less than a family pizza night per month. Yet many ignore it.

> ***Pro-tip***: *Always compare **term insurance** quotes online before buying. A few minutes of research can save lakhs over the policy term.*

Health insurance is another must-have. Medical costs are rising faster than inflation. A hospital stay without insurance can wipe out your savings in one week. And many assume their employer's group insurance is enough—until they resign, retire, or the policy limit is too low.

> ***Pro-tip***: *Choose a policy with cashless hospital networks near your home for faster claims during emergencies.*

Motor insurance is legally mandatory but often underused. If your car meets with an accident and your policy doesn't cover damage to property or third-party liability, you're looking at lakhs of rupees in legal and repair costs.

Home insurance is rarely bought but highly underrated. Imagine a fire, flood, or theft damaging your house or its contents. Home insurance provides peace of mind against nature or negligence.

A case that shows the power of a term plan

Anuj, a 38-year-old software engineer in Pune, was the sole earner in his family. He had taken a ₹1 crore term insurance policy five years ago. Tragically, he passed away due to a sudden illness. While the emotional toll on the family was immense, the term plan ensured financial security. His wife used the funds to pay off their home loan, secure their child's education, and set up a small business.

Without that term plan, the family would have faced debt, distress, and despair.

Mistakes to avoid:

1. Underinsuring: A ₹10 lakh plan might seem big, but it won't last more than a year or two in urban India. Go for at least 10–15 times your annual income.
2. Skipping renewals: One missed premium, and years of protection can vanish.

If insurance is your shield, your emergency fund is your sword. It's the money you pull out immediately when life gets tough. Experts recommend keeping 3–6 months of living expenses in a place that's easy to access but not too easy to spend. That sweet spot includes high-interest savings accounts or liquid mutual funds. Not your stock portfolio. Not your fixed deposits with penalty clauses.

Ravi, a 29-year-old teacher, was great at saving. He invested most of his extra money in equity mutual funds and NPS. But when his mother had an unexpected surgery, he didn't have quick cash. He had to take a personal loan at 14% interest. Had he kept ₹1–2 lakh in a liquid fund, he could've avoided the loan. Investing your emergency fund for high returns defeats its very purpose. The fund is not about growth. It's about instant access with no regret. Use a separate account and nickname it something boring like "Do Not Touch" or "In Case of Fire." It helps reduce temptation. Real Estate: Protection Through Tangibility. Unlike stocks or mutual funds that go up and down on a screen, real estate feels real. It has a comforting solidity. Owning your primary home provides not just emotional comfort but also financial safety. In hard times, not paying rent saves you thousands each month. You can also leverage property by renting part of it or taking a loan against it. But real estate is not without its risks.

Preeti and Arjun bought a flat in Delhi from a builder who promised "all approvals." Turns out, the land title was under dispute. The couple spent years fighting in court, and the flat's value dropped.

Due diligence is everything.

Always verify:

1. Land title and ownership.
2. Approvals from municipal authorities.
3. Encumbrance certificate.

4. Builder reputation (if under construction).
5. Registration papers.

A properly bought home can provide rental income, future resale value, and protection against inflation. But shortcuts can cost you your peace and money.

In Indian households, gold is more than jewellery. It's security in shiny form. During crises, gold can be pledged or sold quickly. It doesn't lose value dramatically and is accepted everywhere. That's why families, especially in rural areas, still trust gold more than banks. But holding too much physical gold has downsides: theft risk, locker fees, and no interest. That's where digital gold or sovereign gold bonds (SGBs) come in. These offer safety, easy liquidity, and in some cases, even 2.5% interest (SGBs). During the COVID lockdowns, Meena's family business faced huge losses. With no income for months, she pledged her wedding jewellery at a bank and got a ₹4 lakh loan with minimal interest. It helped them survive until business picked up.

Gold is not just an adornment—it's your emergency Plan B. Use it wisely. Avoid buying blindly during festivals or promotions. And remember, not all glitter is protection. Jewellery with heavy making charges is less liquid than gold coins or bars. Cryptocurrency is the financial wild west. For some, it's an exciting new way to grow and protect wealth from inflation and currency depreciation. For others, it's a dangerous bubble. The truth lies somewhere in between.

Let's be clear: crypto is not a replacement for emergency funds or insurance. But as part of a well-diversified portfolio, it can serve as a hedge—especially against fiat currency devaluation or geopolitical instability. Bitcoin, for example, has outperformed most traditional assets over the past decade. But its volatility is not for the faint of heart.

> ***Pro-tip***: *Never invest more than 5–10% of your savings in crypto. It is a hedge, not a foundation.*

Shantanu, a 35-year-old data scientist, started investing 5% of his savings in Bitcoin and Ethereum in 2018. By 2021, his crypto portfolio was up 400%. During India's economic slowdown, while his mutual funds stagnated, crypto gave him the confidence to hold on. But he also regretted not booking some profits in time. When crypto crashed in 2022, he saw half of his gains vanish overnight. What saved him? He never invested more than what he could afford to lose.

If you're exploring crypto as protection:

1. Use trusted Indian exchanges or cold wallets.
2. Never keep large amounts on hot wallets (apps that stay connected to the internet).
3. Diversify within crypto (Bitcoin, Ethereum, stablecoins—not meme coins).
4. Declare taxes properly and stay updated on regulations.

Crypto is like fire: controlled, it can protect. Uncontrolled, it can burn everything down.

Today, your money lives in your phone and your inbox. UPI, NEFT, credit cards, and wallets—all convenient but vulnerable.

The more digital we go, the more we need to defend. Cybercrime is not a distant threat. It's happening every day. Phishing links, fake payment requests, fraudulent calls pretending to be bank staff—scammers are getting smarter. One click on a suspicious SMS can empty your account in minutes.

> ***Pro-tip***: *Save bank helpline numbers in your phone. Quick action within the first 30 minutes of fraud can save your money.*

Rekha, a retired schoolteacher, received a call saying her bank account needed re-verification. She was told to share her OTP for KYC verification. Within 15 minutes, ₹95,000 was gone. She had never even signed up for UPI. The fraudster used her PAN and Aadhaar details, easily available online, to create a virtual account.

How can this be prevented?

1. Use two-factor authentication.
2. Never share OTPs, PINs, or account details over the phone, even with someone claiming to be from the bank.
3. Lock your SIM card with a PIN.
4. Use apps like Google Authenticator or Authy for secure logins.
5. Regularly check your bank app settings and linked devices.
6. Set daily UPI limits and enable transaction alerts.

Teach your children and elderly parents about cyber hygiene. One simple rule: if something seems urgent and asks for money or details, pause and verify.

Estate planning, protecting your money after you're gone. Talking about death feels uncomfortable. But if you truly care about your family, you'll plan for what happens when you're not around. Estate planning is not just for the ultra-rich. It's for anyone with a bank account, property, jewellery, or even a phone wallet. A Will ensures your money, house, and belongings go to the people you want. A nominee ensures your spouse or child can access your funds without running to the court. A Power of Attorney helps someone you trust act on your behalf if you're incapacitated.

What Happens Without a Nominee?

Manish died in a car accident. His fixed deposit of ₹18 lakh had no nominee. His wife spent two years in a legal battle to prove her relationship and claim the money. In the meantime, she had to borrow from friends to manage household expenses. Had he filled out one form and added her as a nominee, the money could've been transferred in a week. Think of estate planning as emotional insurance. It doesn't just transfer money; it transfers peace, love, and clarity. Make a Will. Update nominees every year. Store passwords and documents in a secure place. Teach your family how to access them when needed.

Nextis diversification, don't let one basket break everything. There's a saying in finance: "Don't put all your eggs in one basket." Diversification spreads risk across assets so that if one fails, others can protect you.

***Pro-tip**: Use the Rule of Five—hold at least five asset classes to reduce overall risk.*

Imagine an investor who puts all his money into stocks. When markets crash, so does his wealth. Another investor spreads money across:

1. Equity mutual funds
2. Fixed deposits
3. Gold
4. Real estate
5. Liquid funds

Even if one category dips, the others cushion the fall.

Investor A: 100% in mid-cap stocks. Gained 30% in 2020, lost 40% in 2022.

Investor B: 30% in equity, 20% in FDs, 20% in gold, 10% crypto, 20% real estate. Gained 15% in 2020, lost just 5% in 2022, and recovered faster.

Diversification isn't just about safety—it also provides emotional relief. When one asset falls, others rise. You don't feel the panic of a total collapse.

Make your money work in different rooms of the same house.

Your bank isn't just a place to park money. It's the bridge between your earnings and your lifestyle. But it can also become a point of leakage if not managed smartly. Start with reputed banks that are covered under the DICGC insurance—this guarantees up to ₹5 lakh of your deposits in case the bank collapses. Private co-operative banks sometimes don't offer this protection. Joint accounts are helpful in emergencies but can get messy during disputes or separation. Auto-debit instructions for loans or apps must be regularly reviewed.

You'd be surprised how many people pay for things they no longer use—subscriptions, hidden bank charges, locker fees.

Set banking alerts for:

1. Balance drops
2. Suspicious logins
3. ATM withdrawals
4. High UPI spends

Use net banking dashboards to track all your deposits—FDs, RDs, sweep-in accounts. And don't keep all your money in one account. Separate your spending account from your savings. Banking is no longer just about cheques and cash. It's your digital safety vault.

Protect your identity and documents. Your PAN, Aadhaar, and passport are not just ID proofs—they are financial skeleton keys. If stolen, they can be misused to take loans, open bank accounts, and commit fraud in your name.

Harshit, a 30-year-old consultant, found his credit score had dropped mysteriously. After investigation, he discovered a ₹1.5 lakh loan had been taken in his name by someone who had cloned his PAN card. He had no idea until he applied for a car loan.

What can you do?

1. Never share full copies of your documents on public platforms.
2. Use masked Aadhaar copies when needed.
3. Upload sensitive documents to DigiLocker, a government-verified cloud locker.
4. Keep hard copies in a secure place at home—and let your spouse know where.
5. Monitor your credit score every few months via apps like CIBIL or OneScore.

Digital security is as crucial as physical locks on your front door.

Money protection isn't just a solo mission. Imagine building a fortress and then handing the keys to someone who doesn't know what a lock is. That's what happens when you protect your finances but don't involve your family. Every household member—spouse, children, even ageing parents—should have basic financial literacy and a clear understanding of what to do during emergencies.

> ***Pro-tip****: Create a one-page "Emergency Contact Sheet" for your family with all critical numbers and logins.*

Start by creating a simple Emergency File. This can be physical, digital (on DigiLocker or Google Drive), or both. It should include:

1. Insurance policies and claim procedures
2. Bank account details

3. Password manager access
4. Copies of ID proofs
5. List of investments with contact persons

But beyond the file comes the conversation.

Talk openly with your spouse about where money is kept, how bills are paid, what loans exist, and who the financial advisor is (if any). These conversations can feel awkward at first, but are invaluable.

In Bengaluru, 16-year-old Priyanshi noticed a suspicious SMS on her father's phone requesting an urgent bank verification. She stopped him from clicking the link and called the bank instead. It was a phishing attempt. Her awareness came from dinner table discussions where her father had explained cyber scams. When children and spouses are trained, they become part of the protection system. Remember, knowledge shared is safety multiplied.

Let's shift gears from external protection to internal strength. One of the biggest threats to your money isn't out there—it's in your head. It's the impulse to splurge, the greed to double money quickly, the overconfidence to time the market, or the fear of missing out. We've all met someone who lost lakhs in multilevel marketing (MLM) schemes or get-rich-quick plans.

Rahul, a marketing executive, was convinced by a college friend to invest ₹2 lakh in a wellness MLM scheme. "Guaranteed 300% return in 6 months," they said. He didn't ask, "How?" He didn't read the fine print. Six months later, the company disappeared—and so did his money.

Always ask:

1. Who benefits from this?
2. What's the catch?
3. Is this regulated?
4. Can I afford to lose this?

Impulse buying is another leak. Flash sales, influencer ads, and shopping apps are designed to trigger dopamine. But remember: a ₹2000 unnecessary purchase every week becomes ₹1 lakh a year. Protect your future from the whims of your present self. Slow down. Reflect. Walk away. If it's truly valuable, it'll still be there tomorrow.

Technology can be your enemy—or your best financial guard. When used wisely, automation can stop you from sabotaging your savings out of mood swings, late-night cravings, or payday excitement.

Set rules and systems that operate without your permission—but with your best interest in mind. Take the case of Ananya, a corporate employee in Hyderabad. Every payday, ₹5000 is automatically transferred from her main account to a hidden savings account she doesn't touch. She calls it her "Invisibility Fund." It's not linked to her UPI. She doesn't get SMS alerts for it. In two years, she saved ₹1.2 lakh without feeling the pinch.

Here are some brilliant automation ideas:

1. Auto-block debit card after you hit your daily limit.
2. Auto-transfer 10% of income to a separate account.
3. Set alerts for expenses above ₹2000.

4. Use apps that categorise spending (like Walnut, CRED, or Fi).
5. Use UPI for essentials and a different ID for discretionary expenses—you'll instantly know where your money is leaking.

Automation turns discipline into default. Instead of relying on willpower every day, rely on systems that make overspending harder.

Let's go back to the beginning. You've worked hard to earn, smartly to save, and now wisely to protect. Think of your financial life not as a castle made of glass, where one storm shatters everything—but as a fortress. A solid, layered fortress that stands strong, whether life brings rain or fire. Protection isn't about paranoia. It's about peace. You don't need to become a miser or a cynic. But you do need to be mindful, strategic, and one step ahead. Every tool we discussed—insurance, emergency funds, diversification, estate planning, cybersecurity, automation—adds a layer of armour. Alone, each one might not save the day. But together, they form a resilient system.

You've already taken the first step by thinking beyond saving. Now, do one more thing: act.

Here's your mission for this week:

1. Add a nominee to any financial account that doesn't have one.
2. Set up or review your emergency fund.
3. List out your insurance policies and renewal dates.
4. Talk to your family about where important documents are stored.
5. Enable 2-factor authentication on your bank apps.

Just one action will move you toward safety.

Final thought:

"Money is freedom only when it's protected from chaos."

Don't just grow wealth—guard it. Don't just own assets—fortify them. Don't just build a future—defend it like it matters. Because it does.

☑ Key Takeaways From This Chapter

- **Saving is half the story**; protecting your money ensures it survives threats.
- **Three layers of protection**: Security, Stability, and Survivability.
- **Insurance is protection, not investment**—cover life, health, motor, and home.
- **An emergency fund is your financial sword**, providing instant access in crises.
- **Real estate adds tangible safety**, but due diligence is vital.
- **Gold is Plan B security**, with sovereign bonds safer than jewellery.
- **Cryptocurrency is a high-risk hedge**, not a foundation of savings.
- **Cybersecurity protects digital money**—enable 2FA, avoid sharing OTPs, and set limits.

- **Estate planning transfers peace**, not just money—make Wills, add nominees, update regularly.
- **Diversification spreads risk** so one market crash won't wipe you out.
- **Smart banking habits** prevent leaks—alerts, separate accounts, and vigilance.
- **Protect your identity** with masked Aadhaar, DigiLocker, and credit score checks.
- **Family involvement multiplies safety**, ensuring everyone knows what to do in emergencies.
- **Impulse control shields wealth**—avoid scams, MLMs, and unnecessary spending.
- **Automation makes discipline default**, helping you save without constant effort.
- **Protection builds a fortress**, making wealth resilient against life's storms.

✍ Exercises for You

1. Pretend to be an insurance advisor and explain to a family member why term insurance is essential. Teaching out loud builds retention.
2. Label a jar 'Emergency Only' and drop in small notes weekly. Physically seeing it grow builds discipline.
3. Collect and organise your home/property documents in a folder. Tick each document off a checklist.
4. Simulate a phishing attempt with your family and practice how each member should respond.

5. Draw five circles (Stocks, FD, Gold, Real Estate, Crypto) and place your savings percentages inside. Adjust them on paper until balanced.
6. Set up one small automatic transfer today and track it physically in a notebook.

CHAPTER 9

PSYCHOLOGICAL HABITS THAT SAVE MONEY

Training Your Brain to Want Less, Save More, and Grow Fast

Purpose of the Chapter:

To explore how mindset and habits create long-term savings success. This chapter introduces the mental tools, beliefs, and daily actions that unconsciously drive financial well-being—turning good choices into automatic behavior.

What You'll Learn in This Chapter:

- The role of dopamine, willpower, and identity in saving
- Psychological tricks to reduce impulsive or emotional spending
- How "identity-based saving" transforms motivation
- Training your brain through repetition and reward
- Real stories of people who reshaped their lives through mindset

"Your mindset is either spending your money or saving it. Make it your biggest asset."

CHAPTER IX

PSYCHOLOGICAL HABITS THAT SAVE MONEY

The wallet is only a reflection; it is the mind that truly decides whether money multiplies or disappears.

Money, on the surface, seems like a numbers game. Earn this much, spend that much, save the rest. Simple, right? But if it were really that simple, most of us wouldn't be struggling to save. We wouldn't be anxiously checking our bank balances or feeling guilty after a spontaneous shopping spree. The truth is, money problems are rarely just money problems—they're mindset problems in disguise.

What we believe about money—what we fear, desire, assume, or even resent—plays a massive role in how we handle it. This invisible connection between psychology and spending quietly governs our daily decisions, from that second cup of cappuccino to the impulsive online purchase at midnight. If we don't examine these invisible threads, we keep falling into the same spending traps, no matter how much we earn or how many budgeting apps we download. Think about it: Two people with the same income can live drastically different financial lives. One is relaxed, secure, and steadily building wealth, while the other is constantly stressed, overspending, and scrambling to make ends meet. What makes the difference? Often, it's not discipline or opportunity—it's their relationship with money, shaped by years of beliefs, experiences, and emotional habits.

This chapter is all about that invisible relationship. We'll explore how small psychological tweaks—subtle shifts in thinking and daily rituals—can transform the way you interact with money. These habits don't require major sacrifices. In fact, most of them are about creating clarity, not control. They gently nudge your brain into patterns of behaviour that naturally lead to saving, without making you feel like you're missing out on life.

Let's dive deep into these psychological habits and see how they can reshape your financial future—starting with a habit that has stood the test of time: frugality.

Frugality often gets a bad reputation. People think it means being cheap, stingy, or joyless. But that couldn't be further from the truth. At its core, frugality is about intentional spending—choosing value over vanity, simplicity over status, and long-term satisfaction over short-term thrill. Let's say you're tempted to buy a ₹200 coffee every morning before work. It's convenient, it feels luxurious, and it gives you a dopamine boost. But then you decide to invest ₹1200 in a sleek, durable thermal flask. It keeps your home-brewed coffee hot for hours, saves you the daily ₹200, and fits neatly into your routine. In six days, it pays for itself. In a year, you've saved around ₹72,000 without feeling deprived. That's not being cheap. That's being smart.

Frugality shifts your internal dialogue from "I can afford this" to "Is this worth it in the long run?" That single shift can transform your spending habits. You begin to notice how many purchases you make just to fit in, impress, or numb an emotion. Frugality frees you from that cycle. It invites you to build a life where your joy doesn't depend on brand tags or peer validation. A frugal mindset doesn't eliminate pleasure—it refines it. You still enjoy good things, but you enjoy them mindfully. And over time, that mindfulness becomes wealth.

Impulse purchases are like sugar: satisfying in the moment, regrettable in the long run. We've all been there—scrolling through a sale, clicking "Buy Now," and feeling that rush of gratification. But just a few hours later, the excitement fades, and reality sets in. That's because impulsive spending is rarely about need—it's about emotion.

One of the most powerful psychological tools to break this cycle is the "Delay the Purchase" rule. Here's how it works: when you feel the urge to buy something, especially if it's non-essential, don't buy it immediately. Instead, wait 24 to 72 hours. Give your brain time to cool off, reassess, and determine if you really want or need that item.

Take the example of Priya, a 32-year-old graphic designer. She used to make at least three online purchases a week—small things, under ₹1000. But those small things added up to ₹30,000 per year. One day, she made a rule for herself: she'd still add items to her online cart, but she wasn't allowed to check out until at least 48 hours had passed. The result? Most of the time, the excitement faded, and she didn't feel the same urge to buy. Over a year, her savings multiplied, and she felt more in control.

This simple trick creates psychological distance from the urge. It lets the logical part of your brain catch up with the emotional part. And more often than not, you'll realise you never really wanted it—you just wanted the feeling.

Every financial decision is a trade-off. But unless you compare it with something meaningful, you'll never feel the weight of that trade-off. That's where anchoring comes in—a powerful psychological tool where you compare a potential purchase to a bigger, more valuable goal. Let's say you're out with friends, and someone suggests a fancy dinner that will cost you ₹3,000. Before you say yes, imagine your goal: a ₹2,00,000 Goa trip fund. Suddenly, that ₹3,000 isn't just a dinner—it's 1.5% of your dream vacation. That's anchoring in action. Anchoring gives your brain a reference point. It makes invisible costs visible. It connects your day-to-day decisions with your bigger aspirations. Instead of floating in the moment, you ground yourself in purpose.

Think of your top three financial goals—maybe buying a home, funding a child's education, or building an emergency fund. Mentally "anchor" these goals in your mind. Every time you're about to spend on something non-essential, ask yourself: "Is this worth delaying my goal?" Over time, your spending decisions will start to align naturally with your dreams.

The traditional budgeting formula most of us learn is simple: Income – Expenses = Savings. You earn, you spend, and you save whatever is left. But the problem is, there's rarely anything left. Lifestyle inflation eats it up, and our brain justifies every rupee spent. Now flip that equation: Income – Savings = Expenses. This small tweak changes everything. Instead of treating savings like an afterthought, you treat it like rent or electricity—non-negotiable. You decide how much to save first, and live on the rest. This approach doesn't just change your cash flow—it rewires your psychology. It sends a powerful signal to your brain: your future matters. You begin to build psychological safety, knowing your tomorrow is taken care of. That safety reduces anxiety, increases confidence, and creates space for long-term planning.

Let's take the story of Suresh, a school teacher earning ₹50,000 a month. For years, he struggled to save. But once he automated a ₹5,000 transfer to his savings account on salary day, something shifted. He adjusted to ₹45,000 without stress. Within a year, he had ₹60,000 saved and felt more secure than ever.

Saving first isn't about discipline—it's about priority. When you pay your future self first, your present self learns to adapt. And that's a psychological win.

In a world that constantly tells you to want more, striving for "enough" is a radical act. The idea of "enoughness" goes against everything modern consumer culture promotes. Ads tell us we're just one purchase away from happiness. Social media shows curated lifestyles that seem just a little shinier than ours. And quietly, we begin to believe that what we have is never enough. But here's a powerful psychological truth: feeling like you have enough creates space for peace, satisfaction, and… savings.

When you practice enoughness, you stop chasing constant upgrades—newer phones, bigger houses, trendier clothes—and start appreciating what already surrounds you. Try this simple but profound journaling prompt: "What was enough for me five years ago?" You might realise that you lived with fewer clothes, simpler meals, or a smaller home—and you were still content. That reflection alone can shake the illusion that you need more today.

Let's look at Maya, a 29-year-old marketing executive. After three years of rapid career growth and rising income, she noticed her spending had climbed just as fast. But she wasn't any happier. One weekend, she challenged herself to do a "gratitude inventory" of her life. She listed what she already had and loved—a cosy apartment, home-cooked meals, quality time with friends. It made her realise she didn't need to upgrade to feel good—she just needed to recognise herself enough.

Enoughness isn't about stagnation. It's about knowing that contentment doesn't require consumption. And when you anchor yourself in that mindset, your urge to spend impulsively begins to dissolve.

Let's be honest—₹500 doesn't feel like a lot when you're holding it. But if someone told you it costs three hours of your life, would you spend it the same way?

One of the most powerful money-saving habits is thinking of your money in terms of time. Every rupee you earn is time you traded from your life. So when you spend, you're not just spending money—you're spending life. To start, calculate your hourly earning rate. If you earn ₹40,000 per month and work 160 hours (roughly 40 hours/week), your hourly rate is ₹250. Now imagine a ₹1,000 dinner. That's four hours of your life—half a workday—for one meal. This shift changes everything. It transforms frivolous spending into emotionally expensive decisions. You'll think twice before splurging on items that don't deeply matter to you.

Take Rajiv, a software engineer. He began seeing all his non-essential purchases through this lens. That fancy pen? Two hours. That designer t-shirt? Five hours. It made him ask himself, "Is this really worth the time I traded for it?" And most of the time, the answer was no.

When you visualise money as time, it deepens your respect for both. You save more—not because you're forcing yourself—but because the emotional cost of wasting your life energy becomes too high.

Sometimes, to truly appreciate what you have, you need to briefly go without it. That's the psychology behind scarcity simulation—voluntarily creating small periods of "lack" to reset your consumption habits and boost appreciation. This doesn't mean hardship. It means choosing to challenge yourself with short-term, intentional restrictions: a no-sugar week, a no-online-shopping month, or using only public transport for a week. These exercises aren't about punishing yourself—they're about breaking the automatic loop of convenience and comfort that fuels unconscious spending.

Let's take Sneha's case. She noticed that she was spending nearly ₹10,000 a month on food delivery apps. It wasn't just the cost—she felt lazy, unhealthy, and disconnected from cooking. So she set a one-month "no-swiggy" rule. She cooked all her meals at home. Not only did she save ₹9,500 that month, but she also rediscovered joy in cooking, lost a little weight, and felt proud of her discipline.

Voluntary deprivation sharpens your sense of value. When you return to your regular life, your baseline of appreciation is higher. You enjoy things more because you've given yourself a chance to miss them. The trick is to make these challenges feel empowering, not restrictive. Set a reward at the end—maybe a budgeted treat. Over time, these mini-experiments build resilience, creativity, and serious financial muscle.

Have you ever opened an online shopping app after a stressful day—just to browse, just to "feel better"—and suddenly found yourself ₹2000 poorer? If yes, you've experienced emotional spending. This silent money leak is driven not by needs, but by moods: stress, boredom, loneliness, celebration, or even low self-worth.

To overcome it, you need awareness, not willpower. Emotional spending is like a reflex—it kicks in without conscious thought. The first step to breaking it is identifying your emotional triggers. Do you shop more when you're anxious? Do you order food when you're lonely? Do you celebrate good news by spending? One helpful tool is a mood tracker. Every time you feel the urge to spend, pause and write down what you're feeling. Over a week or two, patterns emerge. You'll start seeing that you're not spending on stuff—you're spending for self-soothing. Once aware, you can create new rituals to handle those emotions: journaling, taking a walk, calling a friend, listening to music, or even decluttering. The goal isn't to deny yourself pleasure—it's to disconnect money from mood.

Consider Vinay, who used to shop every Friday night after a tough workweek. Once he realised this was stress-driven, he replaced the habit with a walk and a playlist he loved. Over three months, his bank balance improved, and so did his sense of emotional clarity.

Emotional spending is just a signal—listen to it, and you'll save more than just money. You'll also save your peace.

Want lasting change in your financial habits? Don't start with your budget. Start with your identity. The way you see yourself determines the way you behave. If you see yourself as someone who "just can't save," your brain will subconsciously act to confirm that belief. But if you redefine your identity—say, "I'm someone who makes smart financial decisions"—your actions begin to follow that new script. This is called identity-based change. Unlike goal-based change, which focuses on outcomes, identity-based change transforms your beliefs. When you believe you're a "saver," saving becomes natural, even enjoyable.

You can begin rewiring your identity through daily affirmations and habit stacking. For instance, start each morning by saying, "I'm someone who respects money and uses it wisely." Pair that with a simple action—like reviewing your balance or logging an expense.

Let's revisit Anjali, a freelancer who used to feel ashamed of her poor money habits. Instead of trying to become a budgeting expert overnight, she changed one belief: "I'm someone who tracks expenses every day." That small identity led to a consistent habit. Within six months, she built an emergency fund and called herself, proudly, "a financially responsible person."

Identity change doesn't happen in a week. But once it takes root, it creates self-reinforcing loops. You no longer force yourself to save—you do it because it's who you are.

We have rituals for birthdays, prayers, and even Sunday brunch—but when it comes to money, most of us just wing it. The truth is, mindful money rituals can become one of the strongest psychological anchors for financial growth.

Think of these as small, intentional habits that build your financial self-awareness. Checking your bank balance every morning. Logging your expenses before bed. Review your goals every Sunday. These rituals create a rhythm—a calming, reliable pattern—that removes fear and replaces it with clarity.

Take Rahul and Nisha, a married couple in their 30s. They were always anxious about money, despite both earning decent salaries. But every month ended in stress and overdrafts. They decided to create a Sunday evening ritual: chai, soft music, and a half-hour "money talk." They'd review expenses, update their savings goals, and even plan one fun thing to look forward to. Within three months, not only had their finances improved, but so had their relationship with money and each other.

Money rituals are powerful because they remove shame and secrecy. You face your finances with curiosity, not judgment. Over time, these routines become second nature—just like brushing your teeth. They turn money management from a stressful chore into a grounding practice.

> *And here's a Pro-tip: make it enjoyable. Light a candle, sip your favourite drink, play your favourite playlist. The goal is to build positive associations, so your brain starts looking forward to these moments of financial clarity.*

In today's digital world, spending money has never been easier. Just one tap, swipe, or scan—and it's gone. That convenience may be great for tech, but it's terrible for your bank account. To save more, sometimes you need to intentionally make spending harder. This is called creating friction. It's a behavioural trick that slows down impulsive behaviour by inserting extra steps between your urge and your action. It could be as simple as uninstalling shopping apps, removing saved card details, or setting your UPI pin to something you can't type mindlessly.

Take Meera, a 26-year-old student who found herself overspending ₹12,000/month on beauty products and clothes. Her breakthrough came when she deleted two shopping apps and removed all saved payment methods. Suddenly, buying something meant logging into her laptop, entering her card number, and confirming with an OTP. That friction gave her brain enough time to reconsider. Her spending dropped by half in the first month.

On the flip side, you can reduce friction for saving. Automate monthly transfers to your savings account. Make your investment apps easy to access. Keep a piggy bank visible on your desk for spare change. Make it smoother to save and slower to spend, and you'll find your habits begin to shift—almost effortlessly. Friction doesn't mean restriction. It's simply a pause button for your instincts. And sometimes, that pause is all you need to protect your future.

It might surprise you, but one of the most powerful money-saving habits has nothing to do with budgets, spreadsheets, or bank accounts. It's gratitude. When you regularly practice gratitude, you feel more content with what you already have. And content people don't feel the same hunger to buy more, own more, or prove themselves through purchases. Gratitude is like a psychological vaccine against the disease of consumerism. Research shows that people who keep a daily gratitude journal tend to spend less, save more, and feel more in control of their finances. Why? Because they're less influenced by FOMO (fear of missing out), envy, or the constant "more-is-better" messages we're bombarded with.

Start small. Every night before bed, write down three things you already own that you're grateful for. Your sturdy laptop. The mattress that gives you restful sleep. The old sweater that still feels like a hug. These little acknowledgements shift your focus from what's lacking to what's enough.

Take the example of Kavita, a stay-at-home mom who felt financially insecure despite her husband's stable income. She began a gratitude journal focused only on the material comforts they already had. After two weeks, she noticed a significant drop in her online shopping behaviour. She no longer felt the compulsion to buy, just to feel secure. Gratitude won't magically grow your savings—but it will make you less likely to sabotage them. And that's a transformation worth pursuing.

The human brain loves visuals. That's why dream boards, vision collages, and even motivational screensavers work so well. When you're trying to save or grow money, it helps immensely to see your goals—literally.

Creating a money visualisation board is more than a fun DIY project. It taps into a deep psychological mechanism: when your brain sees something often, it begins to prioritise it. So if you constantly see images of your dream home, your debt-free life, or your child's education fund, those visions start to guide your decisions—even subconsciously.

Let's take Tushar, an entrepreneur who struggled with impulsive spending. He created a collage of his long-term financial goals—pictures of a plot he wanted to buy, the mountain town he dreamed of retiring to, and even a snapshot of his ideal bank balance. He set this collage as his phone's lock screen. Every time he reached for his phone (especially to open a shopping app), he was reminded of his goals. That one-second visual nudge helped him pause—and often resist the temptation.

You can make your board physical or digital. Cut out magazine pictures, print online photos, or use apps like Canva. What matters is that it's personal, vivid, and visible. The goal is to make your future dreams feel as emotionally exciting as today's sales. Because the more real your vision feels, the easier it is to say "no" to distractions and "yes" to your dreams.

If this chapter has shown you anything, it's this: saving money isn't just about numbers—it's about narratives. The stories you tell yourself about money, the emotions you attach to it, and the identity you build around it all shape your financial destiny.

Think of each habit we've explored not as a tip, but as a mental lens—a new way to see your money. Frugality isn't sacrifice; it's power. Delaying purchases isn't a restriction; it's freedom. Anchoring your spending to goals doesn't limit you; it aligns you. Every single mindset shift is a tool to reclaim control—not just over your finances, but over your relationship with life itself.

These habits aren't about forcing yourself into a joyless, spreadsheet-filled existence. They're about building clarity. They help you see through marketing manipulation, emotional traps, and societal pressure. They help you step off the hamster wheel of always wanting more, and build a life where what you have is enough—and still growing.

Here's a final challenge: pick just one habit from this chapter and try it this week. Delay one purchase. Start a gratitude list. Create a vision board. Track your mood when spending. Then, observe—not just your bank balance, but your peace of mind. Because that, too, is wealth.

In the end, protecting your money starts with changing your relationship with it. And that journey begins in the most powerful place of all—your mind.

☑ Key Takeaways From This Chapter

- **Frugality** is not about being cheap; it's about intentional spending and long-term value.
- The **Delay the Purchase Rule** helps reduce impulse spending by adding time for reflection.
- **Anchoring** connects small expenses to big goals, making trade-offs visible.
- Reversing the formula to **Income – Savings = Expenses** prioritises your future self.
- Practising **Enoughness** builds contentment and lowers unnecessary desires.
- Viewing money as **time exchanged** reframes frivolous spending into a life energy cost.
- **Scarcity simulations** reset consumption patterns and strengthen discipline.
- Tracking and tackling **emotional spending** prevent mood-driven money leaks.
- **Identity-based change** helps align self-image with financial discipline.
- **Money rituals** create consistency and reduce anxiety around finances.
- Adding or reducing **friction** can make saving easier and spending harder.
- **Gratitude** is a psychological tool to prevent overconsumption.
- **Visualisation boards** keep your long-term goals emotionally engaging.

✍ Exercises for You

1. Create a 7-day spending journal where you log every purchase and the emotion driving it.
2. Try a 48-hour delay challenge: before buying any non-essentials, wait two days.
3. Build a small gratitude jar: each day, write one thing you already own that you're grateful for and drop it in.
4. Make a vision board with pictures of your top three financial goals and place it somewhere visible.
5. Simulate scarcity: commit to a 'no online shopping' week or a 'cook-at-home only' week.
6. Design a Sunday money ritual with tea, music, and a 30-minute budget reflection session.
7. Calculate your hourly wage and translate 2-3 of your weekly purchases into hours of life spent.

CHAPTER 10

RED FLAGS OF BUDGETING

The Don'ts of Budget Planning – Things You Should Not Do

Purpose of the Chapter:

To guide readers through the common and uncommon mistakes, temptations, habits, and mental traps that quietly or dramatically sabotage their budget plans. This chapter highlights what not to do—those everyday choices that seem small in the moment but carry big consequences.

What You'll Learn in This Chapter:

- Why budgeting without a goal is doomed to fail
- How untracked expenses and emotional spending quietly erode your savings
- The dangers of relying on credit, social pressure, or cashback illusions
- Why reviewing your budget is just as important as creating it
- How to design a budget that actually survives the realities of life
- And most importantly, how to build a personal "Don'ts List" to protect your money from yourself

"A good budget tells you where to put your money. A great budget keeps you from leaking it."

CHAPTER X

RED FLAGS OF BUDGETING

> *Red flags are not stop signs; they are warning signals. Ignore them, and the small cracks in your budget will one day break the dam.*

Budgeting, at first glance, appears to be a purely mathematical endeavour. Numbers in, numbers out, and whatever is left is either your peace of mind or your stress. But any seasoned saver will tell you that real budgeting is more about behaviour than calculators. It's less about how much you earn and more about how you protect what you earn. And often, the greatest danger to your financial plan isn't lack of knowledge or income—it's the small decisions and habits that go unnoticed until they leave a mark.

Many people approach budgeting as a list of things they must start doing: saving more, tracking every rupee, cooking at home, and investing wisely. These are all important. But equally crucial—and often ignored—are the things one must stop doing. The leaks. The temptations. The red flags. Think of budgeting like maintaining a dam. You can keep adding water (income), but if there are holes in the wall (bad habits), the dam won't hold.

Sometimes those holes are obvious—like splurging on a weekend trip without checking your balance. But often, they're invisible until they've already caused damage.

This chapter is about those very traps. The subtle habits that trip us. The invisible mistakes that sabotage even the most well-intentioned budget. Let's walk through the red flags—some common, some surprising—but all very real. Avoiding them might just be the secret weapon your budget needs.

1. Don't Budget Without a Goal

Imagine boarding a train without knowing your destination. You'll get somewhere, sure—but will it be where you wanted to go? That's what budgeting without a goal feels like. Too many people sit with their notepads or apps, create categories, note expenses, and even stick to them for a while—but they still feel aimless. That's because they haven't tied their budget to a purpose.

A goal gives your budget meaning. It answers the question: "Why am I doing this?"

Take, for instance, two friends—Nikhil and Pranav. Nikhil said he wanted to "save money," so he created a strict budget. But a few weeks in, he began to feel deprived. Why cut that coffee? Why not eat out? "What's the point?" he wondered. On the other hand, Pranav was saving with one dream in mind—a 15-day Europe backpacking trip. Every rupee saved was a step closer to that Eiffel Tower selfie. Did he feel deprived of skipping Swiggy? No. He felt powerful.

The difference? Emotion. Goals create emotional anchors. When your savings are tied to something you deeply care about—travel, a house, your kid's education, quitting your job to freelance—you're more likely to stay disciplined. So, before you draft your next budget, pause. Ask yourself: "What's the one thing this budget is helping me achieve?"

2. Don't Rely Only on Memory – Write It Down

We love to think our brains are better than they are. "I remember my expenses," we say, convinced that our mental tally is accurate. But memory, especially when it comes to small day-to-day spending, is a serial liar. It forgets UPI transfers, random online tips, and the bottle of water at the petrol pump. Over a month, these tiny leaks become a flood.

Let's talk about Anjali, a freelance writer. She was confident about her low-spending lifestyle. She hardly shopped, rarely ate out, and worked from home. But one month, she decided to actually write everything down. What she found shocked her. Over ₹3,000 had gone to things she didn't even consider "real spending"—morning chai from the corner stall, UPI payments for snacks, apps she never used but still paid for, random donations, and tip jars.

Our minds are wired to forget things that don't seem significant. But budgeting success lies in tracking *every* rupee, because it all adds up. Use whatever works for you—a pocket diary, a Google Sheet, a budgeting app. The method doesn't matter. The act of recording does. Because when you see where your money is going, you can finally take charge of it.

3. Don't Budget Without an Emergency Buffer

We all know life throws curveballs. Yet somehow, we plan as if everything will go smoothly. That's where budgets break—when they don't make room for the unexpected.

An emergency buffer is like financial armour. It's not luxury—it's a necessity. A medical emergency, sudden travel, job loss, car trouble, broken phone—these events don't ask for appointments. And when they strike, they don't just demand money; they demolish your entire plan if you're not prepared. A buffer fund doesn't need to be big. Start with ₹5,000–₹10,000 and build up to 3–6 months of expenses over time. It should sit separately—untouched unless a real need arises. This "what-if" fund is not optional. It's your safety rope. Budgeting without an emergency buffer is like walking a tightrope without a net. Eventually, everyone slips. The question is—will you fall or bounce back?

4. Don't Touch Savings for Lifestyle Upgrades

Ah, the reward system. "I've been good with money for 3 months. I deserve this new iPhone." It sounds innocent. Harmless, even. But this is how people cannibalise their progress. Your savings are not an ATM. They're your future. Lifestyle upgrades should only happen *after* your savings goals are met—not instead of them. Suppose you must upgrade something; budget for it in advance. Don't sabotage your long-term goals for short-term dopamine. Remember, savings are not a punishment. They're freedom tokens. Each rupee saved is a future stress avoided. Don't sell that peace of mind for a shiny gadget.

5. Don't Fall for Social Media Lifestyle Pressure

Social media can be a beautiful place to find inspiration. But it's also a landmine for envy, insecurity, and overspending. Every scroll brings a new vacation, a fancy dinner, a shopping haul. The danger lies in comparing your unfiltered reality with someone's highlight reel.

> ***Pro-tip:*** *Whenever social media tempts you to spend, remind yourself: 'Their lifestyle is not my budget.*

Consider the story of Mehul and Priya, a newly married couple. One weekend, they saw a friend's Instagram story—a resort stay in Goa, complete with poolside breakfast and a luxury suite. The FOMO hit hard. Within hours, they had booked a similar stay, despite it not fitting their budget. That weekend cost them ₹40,000—financed by credit card EMIs over six months.

Was the trip enjoyable? Yes. Was it worth the financial stress later? Absolutely not.

Comparison is not just the thief of joy—it's the thief of your financial progress. Learn to appreciate others' milestones without turning them into your compulsions. If you want that lifestyle, plan for it. Don't shortcut your budget to match a moment in someone's story. Their picture-perfect weekend may have been sponsored, gifted, or debt-financed. Yours doesn't have to be.

6. Don't Gamble or Day Trade with Budgeted Money

The thrill of making quick money can be intoxicating. The moment someone sees a friend double their investment in crypto or make ₹2,000 in a single day trading stocks, the temptation sets in. But here's the harsh truth—what you don't hear are the thousands of losses, the anxiety, and the regret. When people gamble or day trade with money meant for essentials, it's not ambition—it's sabotage. Budgeted money has a job—it's your rent, groceries, bills, health, and savings. It cannot and should not be risked. If you want to trade or gamble, set aside a very small portion of "play money" that you are 100% willing to lose. But never confuse that with your survival budget.

Money is not a game. Real wealth grows slowly. It doesn't explode overnight—it compounds.

7. Don't Budget for "Ideal" Months – Be Realistic

In January, many people set resolutions—"This year, no eating out. I'll walk to work. No buying clothes for 6 months." While the motivation is commendable, the execution often fails because we budget for our *fantasy selves*, not our *real selves*.

An ideal month where everything goes perfectly—no health issues, no celebrations, no last-minute invites—is rare. So when we build a budget assuming perfection, we're setting ourselves up for disappointment. And when life intervenes—as it always does—we feel like failures. What works better is budgeting for real life. Review your last 3–6 months of spending. Understand your actual habits, not your imagined ones. Include a cushion for unpredictable events. And don't beat yourself up if every line doesn't match your plan. A good budget is flexible—it flows with your life, not against it.

8. Don't Forget Annual or Irregular Expenses

Many people plan their monthly expenses carefully, but still find themselves short of money when annual expenses show up like uninvited guests. Things like car servicing, school fees, insurance premiums, Raksha Bandhan gifts, or even birthday parties—all these come not every month, but they do come. And they can blow your budget sky-high if you're not prepared for it.

Let's look at Ravi and Anusha, a middle-class couple. Every month, they managed their finances tightly. Then in March, their two-wheeler insurance came up—₹4,200. It wasn't accounted for, so it had to come from their grocery and utility budget. That led to a chain reaction of short payments, delays, and stress.

The solution? Sinking funds. This simply means breaking big, irregular expenses into smaller, monthly savings goals. If your insurance is ₹6,000 annually, set aside ₹500 per month. When December comes, it won't be a surprise—it'll be handled. Irregular expenses are *not* irregular in life—they're only irregular in our budgets. The more we prepare for them, the more stable our finances become.

9. Don't Use Credit to Stretch a Broken Budget

Using a credit card or Buy Now Pay Later (BNPL) to "make the month work" is like borrowing from your future self, who already has enough problems. It feels like a temporary fix, but it slowly becomes a habit. And soon, the debt hole deepens.

BNPL and credit cards are not extensions of your income. They are advance payments with strings attached. If you use them, use them strategically—only for emergencies or when you already have a repayment plan in hand. Budgeting means living within your means, not borrowing to pretend everything is fine. Stretching a broken budget only makes the break wider.

10. Don't Ignore the Partner or Family in Budgeting

Money is not a solo sport when you live with others. If you're budgeting for a family, but only you know the plan, expect confusion, friction, and frustration. It doesn't mean you need a board meeting every night—but there must be transparency, teamwork, and clarity.

Consider Rajeev and Manisha. Rajeev handled the finances. He made all the lists, tracked all the expenses, and gave Manisha a grocery allowance. But one month, Manisha went to the market and bought groceries worth ₹7,000. Unknown to her, Rajeev had already placed an online grocery order. That month, they ended up with double stock—and half the budget gone.

Budgeting is like choreography—it works only when everyone is in sync. If one person is saving and another is spending, the net result is zero. Whether it's your spouse, parents, children, or roommates—share the budget. Discuss goals. Assign roles. Money conversations can be awkward, especially in Indian families where silence about finances is normal. But breaking that silence is a game-changer. When the whole team is rowing in the same direction, the journey becomes smoother, faster, and more peaceful.

11. Don't Ignore Mental Health and Emotional Triggers

Budgeting is not just a numbers game—it's an emotional game too. And this is one of the most misunderstood red flags: emotional spending. Many people sabotage their own finances because they haven't recognised how closely their mood and money are connected. Retail therapy is real—and dangerous. Whether it's sadness, stress, rejection, loneliness, or even celebration, emotions often drive spending decisions. If you're not aware of this pattern, you'll continue to make poor financial choices during vulnerable moments.

The solution lies in awareness and replacement. Start tracking not just *what* you spend on, but *why*. Maintain a journal if needed. If you notice you shop more when you're sad or bored, replace that habit with something healthier—a walk, a friend call, meditation, or journaling. Emotions are part of life, but they shouldn't hijack your budget.

12. Don't Budget Without Reviewing

Creating a budget is only half the journey. The real magic happens in the review stage. Think about it—how do you know your plan is working if you never stop to check? Reviewing your budget is like looking at your map during a long trip. You need to make sure you're still on track, or you might be heading in the wrong direction without realising it. A 10-minute review every week or at least twice a month can save you thousands of rupees. It helps you notice patterns, make adjustments, and feel more in control. A budget isn't a "set and forget" tool—it's a dynamic, living system that needs attention.

Start by scheduling a "money review date" with yourself. Maybe Sunday mornings with coffee. Trust me—it'll become your favourite ritual once you see the benefits.

13. Don't Fall for Subscription Traps

We live in the age of subscriptions. OTT platforms, productivity apps, gym memberships, meditation tools, music streaming, cloud storage—everything comes with a monthly charge. And while each

Subscription traps are dangerous because they fly under the radar. The auto-debit happens quietly, and you don't feel the money going out. But in a year, that ₹3,800 becomes ₹45,600. To avoid this, set a calendar reminder every quarter to review your subscriptions. Ask yourself: Am I really using this? Is there a cheaper plan? Can I share a family pack? Do I need it at all? Cutting subscriptions is one of the fastest and least painful ways to declutter your financial life. Keep what adds real value. Cancel the rest without guilt.

14. Don't Be a "People Pleaser" with Money

Social pressure is one of the most underrated money killers. Many people spend—not because they want to—but because they don't want to say "no." This is especially common in cultures like ours, where hospitality, gifting, and "showing up" are signs of love and respect. But when done at the cost of your budget, it becomes financial self-sabotage.

Let's talk about Sameer, who worked in a government office. Over a year, he attended 14 weddings, 9 birthdays, and 6 baby showers. Each event meant gifts, travel, clothes, and monetary contributions. He felt uncomfortable saying no—especially to friends and cousins. By the end of the year, 25% of his income had gone to events he didn't even enjoy.

Being generous is noble. But there's a line between generosity and people-pleasing. If you're afraid to say "I can't afford this," you'll keep sacrificing your own peace for someone else's approval. Start setting boundaries. If a gift is expected but your budget doesn't allow, offer your time, service, or a heartfelt letter instead. Suggest affordable alternatives—a home potluck instead of a restaurant dinner. Practice saying no kindly, but firmly. You don't owe anyone a financial explanation—but you do owe yourself a healthy budget.

15. Don't Chase Every Sale or Discount

Sales are designed to make you feel like you're saving money. But in reality, they often make you spend money you weren't planning to. The psychology is simple: "This thing is ₹2000, but now it's ₹1000—I'm saving ₹1000!" No, you're *spending* ₹1000. Sales trigger FOMO—the fear of missing out. They rush your decision-making and bypass logic. Suddenly, you're buying things you never needed, for occasions that may never come. To avoid this trap, use the 24-hour rule. See something on sale? Wait a day. If you still want it, and it fits in your budget, buy it. Better yet, make a list of things you *actually* need, and only buy during sales from that list. Sales are tools. When used wisely, they save you money. When used impulsively, they drain it.

16. Don't Budget for the Month—Budget by Weeks

A common mistake many people make is planning their expenses based on the full month's salary without dividing it into manageable chunks. This approach sounds logical—after all, we're paid monthly—but human behaviour doesn't work that neatly. When people see a full ₹50,000 or ₹70,000 in their account, they tend to relax. The first 10 days go by in a blur of food orders, new outfits, and impulse purchases. Then comes the end of the month—tight, stressful, and often dipping into savings or credit.

Here's a story that illustrates this perfectly. Rachit, a bank employee in Mumbai, had this cycle down to an art. Every first week, he would treat himself to dinners, small gadgets, and random online purchases. By the 20th, he'd be budgeting down to ₹100. It wasn't that he didn't earn enough. It was that his entire budget was front-loaded.

Eventually, Rachit decided to try something radical: weekly budgeting. He divided his essentials (groceries, fuel, commute, etc.) by 4.3 (average number of weeks in a month). Instead of allocating ₹12,000 for groceries, he allocated ₹2,800 a week. This tiny change made him more cautious, more aware, and surprisingly—it gave him a sense of control. There was less binge-spending and more breathing room at month's end.

Weekly budgeting prevents burnout. It helps you course-correct quickly and provides flexibility. The month feels shorter, more manageable, and your money stretches longer. Budgeting isn't just about control—it's about rhythm. Weekly planning gives your finances a healthy beat.

17. Don't Confuse Cashbacks and Rewards with Savings

It's easy to fall for the illusion of savings through rewards and cashbacks. That little notification—"You just earned ₹300 cashback!"—can feel like a win. But the uncomfortable truth is this: it's not savings if you spend more than necessary to get it. This is how these schemes work. They create a false sense of victory by giving you back a slice of the pie you didn't need to eat in the first place.

True savings happen *before* you spend—not after. If you were already going to make a purchase, and a reward is attached, great. But if the reward *creates* the purchase, it's a loss, not a gain. Don't fall for mathematical illusions. Be a mindful spender, not a discount chaser.

As we reach the end of this chapter, it's worth repeating one simple truth—what you avoid is just as important as what you pursue. A strong financial plan is not just about earning more or saving harder. It's also about guarding yourself against the temptations, patterns, and habits that quietly erode your efforts. Budgeting is often portrayed as this restrictive activity—tight belts, no fun, endless spreadsheets. But in reality, it's a form of self-respect. It's saying: "I care enough about my future to take control of my present."

Each red flag we explored in this chapter may feel small on its own—a skipped review, a missed subscription, an impulsive treat. But just like water carves canyons over time, small financial leaks can destroy decades of progress. Your defence system—your awareness of these red flags—is what keeps your hard-earned money safe. So here's a challenge for you.

Right now, write down your personal list of "Budgeting Don'ts." Not just from this chapter, but from your own life. Maybe it's "Don't check Amazon when I'm bored." Or "Don't lend money without written agreements." Or "Don't order food on Sunday evenings just because I'm lazy." Write them down. Review them every Sunday morning, even if it's just for five minutes. Make it a ritual.

Remember, budgeting isn't about being perfect—it's about being prepared. It's not about restriction—it's about protection. It's not a chore—it's a choice you make every day to create a better life, not just for yourself, but for those who depend on you. Be proud of every rupee you've saved, every temptation you've dodged, every mindful decision you've made. These aren't small wins—they're building blocks of freedom. So stay alert. Stay aware. And always, always keep an eye on the red flags—because the best financial disasters are the ones you avoid altogether.

☑ Key Takeaways From This Chapter

Budget without a goal → leads to aimless saving and quick burnout.

Relying on memory → small untracked expenses snowball into big leaks.

No emergency buffer → one crisis can collapse your entire plan.

Dipping into savings for lifestyle → sabotages long-term financial security.

Social media pressure → fuels envy-driven overspending.

Gambling/day trading with essentials → turns survival money into risky bets.

Ideal month budgeting → unrealistic plans collapse under real-life surprises.

Ignoring annual/irregular expenses → sudden shocks derail stability.

Stretching budget with credit → creates a debt spiral disguised as relief.

Excluding family/partner from planning → leads to confusion and wasted money.

Emotional triggers → moods hijack money decisions.

No budget review → errors repeat unchecked, progress stalls.

Subscription traps → silent drains that accumulate yearly losses.

People-pleasing spending → sacrifices your stability for others' approval.

Chasing sales/discounts → tricks you into spending on non-essentials.

Monthly-only budgeting → overspending early, starving later.

Cashbacks & rewards → illusion of savings that actually increase expenses.

✍ Exercises for You

1. Take a sheet of paper and draw your own 'Budgeting Red Flags' chart. Use red markers to note down your personal money leaks.
2. Role-play with a friend or family member: one plays the 'spender' under peer pressure, the other practices saying 'no' politely but firmly.
3. Print out your last 3 months' bank statement. With a red pen, circle all expenses that fall under these red flags. Discuss what changes you can make immediately.
4. Create 4 envelopes (or use digital folders) and label them 'Week 1–4.' Allocate cash or budget limits into each and practice living week by week.

CHAPTER 11

CHARITY: THE FINANCIAL KARMA

Why Giving is the Secret to Growing — Emotionally, Spiritually, and Financially

In This Chapter:

- The invisible power of giving: how charity changes your mindset
- Emotional returns: how giving heals and fulfils
- Spiritual alignment through financial generosity
- Social capital and community connections
- The wealth loop: how giving often brings surprising returns
- Real-life stories of those who gave and gained
- Why charity is budgeting's hidden pillar
- Giving when you earn less — how little can mean a lot
- Designing a giving habit into your budget
- Legacy giving: your financial footprint on the world

"The value of a man resides in what he gives and not in what he is capable of receiving."

– Albert Einstein

CHAPTER XI

CHARITY: THE FINANCIAL KARMA

> "
> *If you light a lamp for someone else, it will also brighten your path.*

When we talk about money, our minds often go to saving, investing, spending wisely, or growing our income. But there's a powerful and often overlooked aspect of financial health that quietly completes the circle of abundance—**charity**. Giving isn't just a moral act. It's a deeply enriching financial behaviour that shapes our attitudes, disciplines, emotions, and even the practical flow of money in our lives.

People often assume that giving makes you poorer, that handing over hard-earned money leaves a dent in your finances. But the opposite is often true. Giving can open the doors to joy, purpose, and sometimes even unexpected financial blessings. In truth, **charity doesn't reduce your wealth—it fulfils it.** It's the emotional and spiritual balance to the logic of income and expenses. And this chapter will show you why it deserves a permanent space in your monthly budget.

Let's begin with a real story.

A middle-class man in Mumbai named Ashok used to set aside ₹3000 a month as "miscellaneous" in his budget—he never tracked where it went. One day, on a visit to his friend's NGO, he met a shy 10-year-old girl who was bright but struggling to stay in school due to fees. Touched by her story, Ashok decided to commit just ₹1000 a month to her education. Over time, he started receiving progress updates and pictures. That act, just a small slice of his income, gave him a joy he had never experienced with buying gadgets or clothes.

Three years later, Ashok said something simple but profound: "I used to think my money was meant only for me. Now I feel like a small part of it belongs to the world." This emotional shift transformed not just his budget but his relationship with money itself. This chapter is about that transformation.

1. Charity as an Abundance Mindset

When you give, especially when you are not wealthy by traditional standards, you're making a loud declaration: "I have enough to share." That's not just generosity—it's abundance thinking in action.

Most of us are raised with a scarcity mindset. We're told there's never enough—of time, of money, of security. But giving even a tiny amount changes the script. You start feeling in control, no longer a slave to the idea that you're just getting by. You begin to internalise a simple but life-changing belief: **"I have enough."**

Take Meena, a housemaid in Pune who earned less than ₹10,000 a month. Despite her financial hardships, she decided to donate ₹100 every month to an animal shelter nearby. Her reasoning? "If I wait to become rich before helping others, I may never help." Over time, Meena noticed her expenses falling naturally—she began to prioritise essentials and lost interest in small indulgences. Her mindset had shifted from lack to sufficiency.

That's the magic of charity—it's not the size of the gift but the spirit behind it that unlocks abundance. You start trusting that there's enough to go around, and with that trust comes peace, clarity, and smarter decisions. Scarcity creates anxiety. Abundance brings balance.

2. Emotional Wealth: The Feel-Good ROI

While most returns on investment are financial, the return on giving is often emotional—and it's incredibly powerful. Studies show that acts of kindness release dopamine, serotonin, and oxytocin, the "feel-good" chemicals in our brains. It's like nature rewards us for being generous.

When you give, especially to a cause that matters to you, you don't just feel noble—you feel energised, purposeful, and proud. Money that's spent on others, particularly on meaningful causes, brings more long-term happiness than money spent on self-gratification. Financial stability is important, but **emotional wealth**—that deep sense of contentment and purpose—comes from knowing your money has made someone else's life better. Charity is a way to turn currency into kindness.

3. Charity as Financial Discipline

You might be surprised, but planning for charity can actually make you more disciplined with money. It gives your finances a purpose beyond bills and luxuries. When you commit to giving a fixed amount every month—say ₹500 or ₹1000—you naturally learn to cut out impulse buys and unnecessary expenses.

It's like setting a moral guardrail. You start asking better questions: "Do I really need this?" or "Can I skip this outing and use the money for something bigger?" This conscious thinking filters into every part of your spending behaviour.

Take Sneha, a young software engineer in Bangalore. She always struggled with overspending on food deliveries and online shopping. One day, she decided to set a "charity line item" of ₹1000 in her monthly budget. She felt it was a small step, but to make room for it, she had to sacrifice a couple of orders on Zomato each month. Over time, she noticed a surprising trend—her savings went up because she started planning every rupee better.

So yes, **charity creates financial boundaries**, not chaos. When you consciously make space for others in your budget, you gain control over your own habits. It turns your budget into a tool for empathy, not just calculation.

4. Building Karma: The Spiritual ROI

In India, charity is not just a good deed—it's a spiritual duty. Whether you call it **daan**, **zakat**, **seva**, or **tithing**, nearly every Indian religion encourages the idea of giving as a path to purity and balance. When we give without expecting anything in return, we generate **good karma**—a kind of spiritual energy that brings peace, grace, and sometimes even unseen blessings. Whether or not you believe in karma, the principle is clear: **when you put good out into the world, good tends to find its way back to you.** Charity strengthens the unseen threads that connect us all. And that connection can sometimes be more protective than an insurance policy.

5. Tax Benefits of Donations (India-Specific)

Now let's talk practical. If you need a tangible, numbers-based reason to give, here's one: **you can reduce your taxable income by donating to approved charities.** Under **Section 80G** of the Indian Income Tax Act, contributions to registered charitable organisations can give you tax deductions—sometimes even up to 100%.

Let's break it down with an example. Pooja, a salaried employee in Delhi, earns ₹9 lakh a year. She donates ₹10,000 annually to an NGO that supports education for girls. Because the NGO is registered under 80G, she can claim a 50% deduction. So, ₹5000 of her income becomes non-taxable.

Of course, you'll need to keep proper documentation—receipts with the PAN of the organisation, and ensure the NGO is eligible under 80G. But with a little planning, **you can support great causes and pay less tax.** That's a financial win-win.

So giving isn't just about losing money—it can smartly reduce what you owe the government, while also letting your money make a difference. It's the best form of budget reallocation.

6. Time as Charity: Volunteering for Value

Sometimes, the wallet may be tight, but the heart is full—and that's when **time becomes the most valuable donation** of all. Volunteering your time, skills, or even attention can be a beautiful form of charity. Not only does it build empathy and strengthen communities, but it also enriches your own personal growth.

Think about the case of Ritesh, a young IT professional in Hyderabad. His salary barely covered rent, food, and a student loan. Instead of waiting for a promotion to start giving, he joined a weekend teaching program in slum areas organised by a local NGO. For two hours every Saturday, he taught basic math and English to children who had never seen the inside of a tuition class.

This experience changed his life. He became more patient, learned to manage his time better, and realised how fortunate he was. In fact, he often says those kids taught him more than he ever taught them.

Volunteering cultivates gratitude. It makes you aware of the luxuries you take for granted and inspires you to live more consciously. It's also a great networking tool—you meet people with shared values, build leadership skills, and gain insights that money could never buy. Charity isn't always about cheques; sometimes, it's about showing up.

7. Giving as a Family Value

Imagine growing up in a home where charity wasn't just discussed but practised. Where birthdays included giving toys to an orphanage, or festivals meant sharing meals with the underprivileged. Such values shape children not just into givers, but into grounded, empathetic human beings.

Teaching charity within the family is a way to **raise emotionally intelligent children** who understand that happiness grows when shared. One simple way is to keep a "charity jar" at home—everyone drops in a little from their pocket money, salary, or festive gifts. At the end of the month, the family decides together where to donate. **Family charity rituals** don't just teach children about compassion; they help reduce materialism. When kids learn the joy of giving, they become less fixated on what they "don't have" and more focused on what they can do.

8. Micro-Charity: Everyday Opportunities

Many people believe charity must be grand or organised. But the truth is, **small, spontaneous acts of kindness** are just as powerful. You don't need a foundation or a spreadsheet to make a difference—you just need a heart that notices.

Buying a bus ticket for someone short on change, handing over ₹20 to a tired construction worker, paying for someone's medicine online—these are all examples of micro-charity. Small, unplanned, but deeply human.

Take Kirti, a homemaker in Surat. Every time she goes grocery shopping, she buys an extra packet of biscuits, sanitary napkins, or fruits for her building's security guards. Over time, the guards began calling her "Maa." That ₹50 gesture became a bond, a relationship.

Micro-charity works because it's rooted in **presence**—you see a need, and you respond. You're not solving the world's problems, but you are making someone's moment better. And that moment adds up in someone's life.

And here's the beautiful irony—often, it's not the receiver who remembers forever. It's the giver. That small act becomes a story you carry, a memory that lights up your day. Charity is not always planned. Sometimes, it's simply **being kind when no one expects it**.

9. Minimalism Through Generosity

In a world of consumerism and fast fashion, it's easy to keep accumulating—more clothes, more gadgets, more décor. But every time you **give away something useful**, you're not just decluttering your space—you're decluttering your mind.

Charity and minimalism go hand in hand. When you donate clothes you haven't worn in six months, or books you've read but won't re-read, you're not just helping others. You're freeing yourself from the psychological weight of possessions. You make space—for peace, for clarity, for better choices. When you give away excess, you begin to recognise what is truly essential. **Charity teaches you to value people over possessions.** And in that mindset shift, your finances benefit, your home breathes easier, and your heart feels lighter.

10. Skill-Based Charity: Give What You Know

Not everyone can donate money, but everyone knows something worth sharing. **Skill-based charity** is one of the most underrated but impactful ways to give. If you're a teacher, coach. If you're an artist, paint walls at a children's home. If you're good with finances, teach budgeting to women's self-help groups.

Take the story of Mr Kulkarni, a retired banker from Nashik. He began volunteering with SHGs (self-help groups) in nearby villages. He taught rural women the basics of saving, avoiding loan traps, and starting micro-businesses. Over four years, many of his students became independent income earners. One even started her own tailoring training centre.

That's the power of giving what you know. It creates **multiplying ripples**—you empower one person, who then empowers ten more. It's also deeply satisfying. You realise that your years of learning have a purpose beyond your paycheques.

Everyone has something they can teach or offer. Whether it's marketing, cooking, Excel, yoga, or soft skills—your knowledge could be someone else's lifeline. Charity isn't always financial—it's **offering your wisdom without a price tag.**

11. Giving Without Expectation: Letting Go of Ego

True charity lies not just in the act of giving, but in how you give. The purest **form of giving is silent**, done without any need for recognition or praise. This kind of charity not only helps others—it **cleanses the ego**. When you give silently, you're not investing in social capital—you're investing in humility. You shift from "Look what I did" to "I did what was right." And that inner shift softens the craving for prestige, which is often one of the biggest drains on money.

Charity becomes a **practice in detachment**, a way to let go of the need to be seen or praised. And ironically, that very act makes you stronger, calmer, and richer—on the inside where it counts most.

12. Charity as a Circle: What Goes Around…

Have you ever heard someone say, "I once helped them, and years later, they helped me back"? Charity often works in mysterious, circular ways. You plant a seed, and the fruit comes back—sometimes through people, sometimes through opportunities, sometimes through peace of mind. Giving doesn't guarantee returns. But **it often activates invisible support systems**. People who give are remembered, referred to, supported, and helped in quiet ways. And even if nothing ever "comes back," the act itself builds inner wealth—trust, resilience, perspective. Giving is a circle. And in that circle, **you're never alone**.

At the end of the day, charity isn't about your bank balance. It's about your **heart balance**. You don't have to wait until you're rich to start giving. Start where you are, with what you have—even if it's just ₹10 or ten minutes.

Giving changes your relationship with money. It transforms money from something to protect into something that protects others. That shift changes everything—it builds discipline, humility, empathy, abundance, and purpose. Make charity a

fixed item in your budget, not an afterthought. Whether it's ₹100, ₹1000, or a few hours a week, it counts. As the saying goes, "**The hands that give are never empty.**" And that's not just a moral truth—it's a financial one too.

☑ Key Takeaways From This Chapter

- **Charity builds an abundance mindset**, you start believing 'I have enough to share.'
- **Giving creates emotional wealth**; the joy of helping is a lifelong ROI.
- **Charity enforces financial discipline**; it helps cut unnecessary spending.
- **Donations offer tax benefits**, support causes while reducing your tax burden.
- **Time and skills are powerful donations too**; volunteering matters as much as money.
- **Family charity rituals build values**; they raise empathetic, grounded children.
- **Micro-charity makes a daily impact**; small acts of kindness add up.
- **True giving is without expectation**; charity cleanses ego and builds humility.
- **Charity completes the circle of abundance**: what goes around, often comes around.

Exercises for You

1. Set aside ₹100 this week and give it in a way that feels meaningful. Reflect on how it felt.

2. Donate one useful household item you haven't touched in six months.
3. Volunteer two hours of your time for any cause near you—teaching, helping, or simply listening.
4. Start a small 'charity jar' at home—drop in coins daily and decide monthly where it goes.
5. Write down three skills you could teach or share for free—then find someone to pass them on to.

This is Not The End.

When you first picked up this book, maybe you were curious, maybe you were frustrated, or maybe you were downright desperate for answers about where your salary disappears every month. You began a journey not just into budgeting, saving, and financial planning, but into something much bigger: a new relationship with money and yourself.

Now, as you reach this final chapter, I want to remind you of one thing: this is not the end. In fact, if you've walked alongside me through the days, strategies, stories, and exercises in this book, this is only the beginning of a richer, calmer, and more purposeful life with money.

The truth about money is that it never really stops moving. Salaries come in, bills go out, investments grow, emergencies appear, desires tempt us, and responsibilities evolve. Money is not static. And so, your financial discipline is not a one-time event. It is a living, breathing practice that grows with you, adapts with you, and walks beside you for the rest of your life.

Let's pause for a moment to appreciate how far you've come.

You started at the very beginning with pre-planning—those quiet, often overlooked days at the end of the month where the groundwork for everything else is laid. Then you moved through payday planning, learning not to let the thrill of a fresh salary sweep you into reckless spending. You learned to design a detailed budget, plan your groceries with the sharpness of a French chef, and keep your household finances neat with financial housekeeping.

You explored monthly challenges that inject excitement into saving, discovered the power of a mid-month reset, and understood why protecting your savings is just as important as earning them. We even dug deep into psychological habits—those invisible mental forces that shape your financial destiny—and recognised the red flags of budgeting, the traps that silently sabotage progress.

We discussed charity and financial karma, a reminder that money is not just for keeping but also for circulating, sharing, and uplifting others. And now, here we are, tying the threads together.

That is a journey worth celebrating. But it doesn't end here.

The Myth of Finality

Too often in life, we treat achievements as endpoints. Graduated from school—done. Get married—done. Buy a house—done. Save a certain amount—done. But life doesn't work that way, does it? Every milestone is simply a door to the next stage.

Financial management is no different. You may feel you've "mastered" budgeting, or maybe you still feel shaky and unsure. Either way, the truth is that there will never be a perfect, final system. Life will always throw changes at you: a promotion, a job loss, marriage, children, medical emergencies, inflation, investments, and retirement. Each of these will force you to adapt your financial plan.

That's why I titled this chapter "This Is Not the End." Because what you've built through this book is not a rigid set of rules, but a flexible mindset. A way of thinking. A way of living.

Think of this: the moment you start managing your salary with intention, you are no longer just working for money. Money starts working for you. And that shift is where your story truly begins.

Imagine your future self, five years from now. You've consistently followed the habits in this book—allocating funds on payday, resetting mid-month, guarding your savings, and checking your red flags. Slowly but surely, you've built up a cushion of savings, maybe some investments, maybe even a down payment for a home or funds for a dream trip. The stress that once came every time your salary arrived and disappeared? Gone. In its place: control, clarity, and confidence.

This is not a fantasy. It's a direct consequence of your daily discipline. And the best part? You don't need to be a financial genius. You don't need luck or lottery tickets. You just need consistency.

And so, your financial story is not about the end of your salary on the 30th of the month. It is about how you stretch, grow, and multiply every rupee to serve your life goals.

The Ripple Effect

Money habits are contagious. When you transform your financial life, the effects don't stop with you. They ripple outward into your family, your friends, your community.

Think about it:

When you stop living paycheck to paycheck, your family experiences less stress. When you save consistently, you create opportunities for your children. When you share wisely through charity, you inspire generosity in others.

When you resist consumerist traps, you model responsible living.

One disciplined individual can change an entire household. One household can influence a circle of relatives. One community can set new cultural standards. That's how revolutions in money management begin—not in government offices or banks, but in the living rooms of ordinary people who decide to take control.

So, as you continue beyond this book, remember: your actions are not just for you. They are seeds planted in the minds of everyone watching you.

Building a Legacy Beyond Money

Here's a hard truth: money alone doesn't make you rich. It's what you do with it that creates wealth. Wealth is measured not just in bank balances but in time, freedom, peace of mind, and impact.

Your financial discipline allows you to buy back time—less overtime, fewer desperate side hustles, more evenings with your family. It grants you freedom—the ability to say no to toxic jobs or unnecessary expenses. It gives you peace of mind—no more sleepless nights worrying about bills. And most importantly, it gives you impact—the ability to leave behind a legacy of wisdom, values, and stability for those who come after you.

Legacy is not about leaving behind a fortune; it's about leaving behind a framework. If your children grow up seeing you budget wisely, save consistently, and give generously, they will inherit something far more valuable than cash: financial discipline as a family tradition.

Now, let me be honest: you will stumble. No matter how disciplined you are, there will be months when emergencies derail your budget, when emotions overrule logic, or when life simply feels too heavy to keep track of expenses.

And that's okay.

The goal is not perfection—it is persistence. Every time you slip, you have the power to restart. Remember the mid-month reset we talked about? That principle applies to life as well. Don't wait for January 1st, or for the next salary cycle, or for the "right time." Restart today, restart tomorrow, restart whenever you fall.

Discipline is not about never failing. It is about failing, forgiving yourself, and beginning again.

Before we close, let's gather the essential tools you'll carry with you from this journey. Think of them as your financial compass:

Awareness – Always know where your money is going.

Pre-Planning – Anticipate expenses before they arrive.

Payday Discipline – Divide your income the moment it comes.

Budgeting – Give every rupee a purpose.

Flexibility – Adjust when life changes.

Resets – Pause, reflect, and correct mid-way.

Protection – Guard your savings from impulse and temptation.

Mindset – Remember that habits matter more than amounts.

Generosity – Share a portion to create joy and balance.

Legacy Thinking – Build systems, not just savings.

If you hold on to these ten tools, you will never truly be lost, no matter how unpredictable your financial journey becomes.

So here we are, at the final words of this book. But unlike most endings, this one doesn't close the story—it opens it.

Tomorrow, your salary will still come. Bills will still knock. Temptations will still whisper. But now you are armed with more than money. You are armed with clarity, awareness, and discipline.

Tomorrow is your opportunity to live differently. To prove that money no longer controls you—you control it. To show that financial peace is not reserved for the rich, but for the disciplined. To live a life where wealth is not just in your bank account, but in your mind, your heart, and your habits.

And remember, whenever you feel lost, whenever you feel like slipping back into old ways, just turn to the title of this chapter and remind yourself:

This is not the end. It's the beginning of the rest of your financial life.

JARGONS

50-30-20 Rule – A budgeting framework dividing income into 50% needs, 30% wants, and 20% savings/investments.

Auto-debit – A facility where payments (like EMIs or bills) are deducted automatically from your bank account.

Auto-renewal – Automatic continuation of a subscription or service unless manually cancelled.

Avalanche Method – A debt repayment method where high-interest loans are paid off first to save money overall.

Bank Statement – A monthly record from your bank showing credits, debits, and balances.

Budgeting Rule – Any structured guideline for dividing income (such as the 50-30-20 rule).

Buffer Fund – Extra money set aside as a cushion for small, unplanned expenses.

Burnout – Mental and physical exhaustion, often due to overwork or poor money management **stress.**

Cash Envelope Method – A budgeting system where money is physically separated into envelopes by category.

Cash Flow – The movement of money in and out of your account—income versus expenses.

Cashback – A reward where a percentage of money spent is returned to you after a transaction.

Cold Wallet – Offline storage for cryptocurrencies, considered more secure than online storage.

Credit Score – A number that represents your creditworthiness and impacts loan approvals.

Crypto – Short for cryptocurrency, digital assets like Bitcoin or Ethereum are used as money or investment.

CTC (Cost to Company) – The total annual salary package including benefits, bonuses, and allowances.

Digital Gold – Gold purchased and stored electronically, without needing physical possession.

Digital Wallet – An app-based tool (Paytm, Google Pay, etc.) for storing and spending money digitally.

Diversification – Spreading investments across different assets to reduce risk.

Down payment – An upfront amount paid when buying assets like a house or car, before taking a loan.

ELSS (Equity-Linked Savings Scheme) – A tax-saving mutual fund that invests in equities.

EMI (Equated Monthly Instalment) – Fixed monthly payments made to repay loans.

Emotional Spending – Spending driven by feelings like stress, boredom, or excitement rather than need.

Emergency Fund – Savings kept aside to cover unexpected life events like job loss or hospital bills.

EPF (Employees' Provident Fund) – A retirement savings scheme where employees and employers contribute monthly.

Estate Planning – Preparing how your assets will be managed or passed on after death.

ETF (Exchange-Traded Fund) – An investment fund traded like stock but holding multiple securities.

Financial Discipline – The habit of controlling spending, saving regularly, and avoiding debt traps.

Financial Karma – The belief that giving (charity) brings both emotional and financial benefits.

Financial Literacy – Understanding money concepts like saving, investing, and debt management.

Fixed Deposit (FD) – A safe investment where money is locked for a fixed period with fixed returns.

Fixed Obligations – Non-negotiable monthly expenses such as rent, EMIs, and insurance.

Guilt-free Spending – Money spent on wants after essentials and savings are covered, without regret.

Income Stream – A source of money earned, such as salary, freelancing, or passive income.

Inflation – The rise in prices over time that reduces the value of money.

Interest Rate – The percentage charged on loans or earned on deposits.

Late Fee – Penalty charged for missing a bill or EMI payment deadline.

Lifestyle Inflation – Spending more as your income grows, often preventing savings growth.

Liquid Fund – A mutual fund offering quick access to money while earning moderate returns.

Minimum Balance – The lowest amount required to be maintained in a bank account to avoid penalties.

Mutual Fund – A pool of money from investors used to buy a diversified set of securities.

Net Salary – The actual take-home salary after taxes and deductions.

NSC (National Savings Certificate) – A government savings scheme with fixed returns and tax benefits.

Overdraft – A facility allowing you to withdraw more money than you have in your bank account, with interest.

Overspending – Spending beyond your budget or means.

Payday Sales – Retail or e-commerce discounts offered around salary credit dates.

Portfolio – The collection of financial investments (stocks, bonds, funds) owned by an individual.

PPF (Public Provident Fund) – A government-backed savings plan with tax benefits and long-term returns.

Recurring Deposit (RD) – A savings account where a fixed sum is deposited monthly, earning interest.

Red Flags – Warning signs of poor financial habits or budgeting mistakes.

Salary Slip – A document showing salary details, deductions, and net pay.

Savings Account – A basic bank account where money is stored safely with a small interest.

Side Hustle – An additional source of income apart from a regular job.

Sinking Fund – A fund saved for specific future expenses like vacations, weddings, or repairs.

SIP (Systematic Investment Plan) – Regular small investments into mutual funds to build wealth gradually.

Snowball Method – A debt repayment method where the smallest debts are paid first to build momentum.

Sovereign Gold Bonds (SGBs) – Government securities linked to gold, offering interest and capital safety.

Spending Habit – A recurring pattern of how someone typically spends money.

Subscription Trap – Losing money to forgotten or unused recurring subscriptions.

Tax Deduction – Amounts reduced from taxable income, lowering your tax liability.

Tax Planning – Managing finances to reduce tax payments legally through savings and investments.

Tax-Saving Instruments – Investments like PPF, ELSS, or insurance that provide tax benefits.

Term Insurance – A life insurance policy that provides coverage for a fixed time at affordable premiums.

Treasury Bills – Short-term government securities used as safe investment options.

UPI (Unified Payments Interface) – A digital payment system in India for instant bank transfers.

UPI Pin – A secure code required to complete UPI transactions.

Variable Expense – Costs that change month to month, such as groceries or fuel.

Variable Pay – Part of the salary based on performance, like incentives or bonuses.